TOP
100
POULTRY DISHES

TOP 100 POULTRY DISHES

SAFEWAY/GOOD HOUSEKEEPING

Published exclusively for
Safeway
6 Millington Road, Hayes, Middlesex UB3 4AY
by Ebury Press
A division of Random House
20 Vauxhall Bridge Road
London SW1V 2SA

First published 1993

Edited by Felicity Jackson and Carol McGlynn
Designed by Peartree Design Associates
Special photography by Ken Field
Food stylist Kerenza Harries
Photographic stylists Sue Russell and Suzy Gittins

The paper in this book is acid-free

Typeset by Textype Typesetters, Cambridge
Printed in Italy

ISBN 0 09 182103 7

COOKERY NOTES

All spoon measures are level unless otherwise stated.

Size 2 eggs should be used except when otherwise stated.

Granulated sugar is used unless otherwise stated.

The oven should be preheated to the required
temperature unless otherwise stated.

Contents

FOREWORD

TOP 100 POULTRY DISHES is one of a popular new series of colourful and practical cookery books created exclusively for Safeway customers. It contains 100 *Good Housekeeping* recipes designed to make full use of Safeway's extensive range of poultry cuts.

The Good Housekeeping Institute is unique in the field of food and cookery, and every recipe has been created and double-tested in the Institute's world-famous kitchens, using readily available ingredients.

There are recipes to suit all occasions, from quick snacks, supper dishes and salads to barbecue and picnic ideas. For entertaining, there is a range of starters and special occasion main meals plus spectacular dishes for festive occasions.

COOKERY EDITOR
GOOD HOUSEKEEPING

DUCK AND ORANGE TERRINE

SERVES 8-10

1.8 kg (4 lb) oven-ready duckling
335 g (12 oz) belly of pork, skinned and boned
115 g (4 oz) lamb's liver
1 onion, skinned and quartered
2 oranges
1 garlic clove, skinned and crushed
salt and pepper
½ × 5 ml tsp ground mace
1 × 15 ml tbs chopped fresh parsley
2 × 15 ml tbs sherry
½ × 24 g packet aspic jelly powder
celery leaves, to garnish (optional)

1. Prepare two days ahead. Discard the skin and fat layer from the duckling. Cut away the breast portions and set aside. Remove rest of flesh; you will need about 335 g (12 oz).
2. Finely mince the duckling flesh with the pork, liver and onion. Grate in the rind of one orange. Segment this orange, removing the membrane, over a bowl to collect any juice. Cut the segments into small pieces.
3. Combine the meat mixture with the orange juice and segments, garlic, seasoning, mace, parsley and sherry. Press half the mixture into a 1.2 lt (2 pt) terrine. Lay the duck breast portions on top and spread remaining mixture over them.
4. Cover the dish and place in a roasting tin half filled with boiling water. Cook at 160°C/325°F/Gas Mark 3 for 3 hours. Place a weight on top of the pâté and refrigerate until cold. Scrape off any solidified fat and drain away the juices.
5. Make up the aspic jelly to 300 ml (10 fl oz) with water, according to the packet instructions. Garnish the pâté with slices of the remaining orange and celery leaves. Spoon the aspic over when it is nearly set. Leave at room temperature for 30 minutes before serving.

Duck and Orange Terrine

Layered Turkey and Ham Terrine

SERVES 8–12

12 streaky bacon rashers, rinded
450 g (1 lb) boneless pork sparerib
225 g (8 oz) pig's liver
115 g (4 oz) fresh white bread, crusts removed
50 g (2 oz) can anchovy fillets, soaked in milk for
  20 minutes and drained
finely grated rind and juice of 1 lemon
4 × 15 ml tbs brandy
50 g (2 oz) shelled pistachio nuts, chopped
1 × size 3 egg, beaten
salt and pepper
225 g (8 oz) boiled ham, thickly sliced
225 g (8 oz) turkey breast fillet, skinned and
  thickly sliced

1. Stretch the bacon rashers with the flat of a large knife. Use to line the base and sides of a 1.2 lt (2 pt) soufflé dish or mould. Set aside.
2. Mince or process the pork, liver, bread and anchovies together. Turn into a bowl and add the lemon rind and juice, the brandy, pistachio nuts, egg and seasoning to taste. Mix well to combine all the ingredients evenly together.
3. Put one-third of the minced mixture in the lined soufflé dish and press down well. Cover with half of the ham and turkey slices. Put another third of the minced mixture in the dish, press down well, then cover with the remaining ham and turkey slices. Top with the remaining minced mixture and press down well.
4. Cover the dish with foil, place in a roasting tin half filled with boiling water and bake at 160°C/325°F/Gas Mark 3 for 2 hours.
5. Carefully drain off the fat and cooking juices, then cover with a plate or saucer and put heavy weights on top. Leave to cool, then chill in the refrigerator overnight.
6. Turn the terrine out of the dish onto a board or serving plate and cut into slices to serve.

Chicken Terrine

SERVES 8

1.4-1.8 kg (3-4 lb) chicken, with giblets
225g (8 oz) belly pork, cut into chunks
2 onions, skinned and quartered
2 garlic cloves, skinned and crushed
2 × 15 ml tbs chopped fresh parsley
2 × 5 ml tsp chopped fresh tarragon
grated rind and juice of 1 small lemon
1 × size 3 egg, beaten
salt and black pepper
bunch of watercress

1. Reserve the liver and heart from the chicken giblets. Using a sharp, pointed knife, remove the breast meat from the chicken and cut it into neat strips; set aside. Remove all the remaining meat from the chicken carcass. (The bones and skin may be used to make good stock.)
2. Mince or process the chicken meat with the chicken liver and heart, the pork and the onions. Put the mixture in a bowl and mix in the garlic, herbs, lemon rind and juice, and the egg. Add seasoning and mix well.
3. Grease a 1.2 lt (2 pt) terrine. Pack half the mixture into it and lay the reserved strips of chicken breast on top. Season the strips.
4. Cut off 2.5 cm (1 in) of the watercress stalks, chop the remainder finely and scatter over the chicken strips. Cover with the remaining minced mixture, packing it down neatly.
5. Cover the terrine with foil and a lid. Pour 2.5 cm (1 in) hot water into a roasting tin, stand the terrine in it and cook at 160°C/325°F/Gas Mark 3 for 2 hours.
6. Remove from the oven, drain off the liquid and place weights on top of the foil while the mixture cools. Remove the weights just before serving and cut the chicken terrine into slices.

Layered Turkey and Ham Terrine

CHICKEN LIVER AND WALNUT PÂTÉ

SERVES 8

2 × 15 ml tbs oil
565 g (1¼ lb) chicken livers, trimmed
1 small onion, skinned and finely chopped
1½ × 5 ml tsp dried tarragon
2 garlic cloves, skinned and crushed
275-335 g (10-12 oz) unsalted butter
1½ × 15 ml tbs brandy or sherry
150 g (5 oz) walnut pieces, toasted
5 × 15 ml tbs double cream
salt and pepper

1. Heat the oil in a large pan and sauté the livers, onion, tarragon and garlic for 3-4 minutes or until well browned. The livers should still be slightly pink in the centre. Stir in 225 g (8 oz) butter, the brandy or sherry and 115 g (4 oz) walnuts. Mix until evenly blended, then leave to cool slightly.

2. Put the liver mixture in a blender or food processor and process with the double cream until smooth. Season to taste. Push the mixture through a fine sieve, then spoon into a serving dish. Refrigerate for at least 1 hour to set.

3. Melt the remaining butter. Roughly chop the remaining walnuts and sprinkle them over the surface of the pâté. Spoon over the melted butter to cover the pâté completely. Refrigerate again to set. The pâté will keep in the refrigerator for about a week.

Chicken and Avocado Mousses

Chicken and Avocado Mousses

SERVES 8

300 ml (10 fl oz) chicken stock
1 × 15 ml tbs gelatine
2 ripe avocados
juice of ½ lemon
225 g (8 oz) cooked chicken, minced or
    very finely diced
bunch of salad onions, trimmed and
    very finely chopped
1 × 5 ml tsp Worcester sauce
pinch of cayenne pepper
salt
150 ml (5 fl oz) double cream
150 ml (5 fl oz) thick mayonnaise
fresh parsley sprigs, to garnish

1. Place the stock in a bowl and sprinkle the gelatine over it. Stand the bowl over a saucepan of hot water and heat gently until dissolved. Leave to cool.
2. Halve, stone and peel the avocados. Mash the flesh with the lemon juice (to prevent the avocados discolouring).
3. Fold the chicken into the avocados with the salad onions, Worcester sauce, cayenne pepper and salt to taste. Stir in the cooled gelatine.
4. Whip the cream until thick, then fold into the chicken and avocado mixture with the mayonnaise. Taste and adjust seasoning.
5. Turn the mixture into eight lightly oiled 115 ml (4 fl oz) moulds, cover and refrigerate for 4 hours until set.
6. Unmould and serve immediately (to prevent the avocado discolouring), with parsley sprigs to garnish.

VARIATION Serve the mousses with a red pepper sauce. Grill 1 large, seeded pepper until the skin blackens, allow to cool, then skin. Chop the pepper and put into a food processor or blender with 150 ml (5 fl oz) single cream, 1 × 15ml tbs lemon juice, salt and pepper and process until smooth. Pour into a small pan and cook over a gentle heat until the sauce is glossy and thick. Allow to cool.

Potted Chicken with Tarragon

SERVES 6-8

1.4 kg (3 lb) oven-ready chicken
3 × 15 ml tbs dry sherry
1 × 15 ml tbs fresh chopped tarragon or
    1 × 5 ml tsp dried
50 g (2 oz) butter
1 onion, skinned and chopped
1 carrot, peeled and chopped
salt and pepper
fresh tarragon sprigs, to garnish

1. Place the chicken in a flameproof casserole with the sherry, tarragon, butter, vegetables and seasoning. Cover tightly and cook in the oven at 180°C/350°F/Gas Mark 4 for about 1½ hours.
2. Lift the chicken out of the casserole and cut off all the flesh, reserving the skin and bones. Coarsely mince the chicken meat in a food processor or mincer.
3. Return the skin and broken up bones to the casserole and cover with water. Boil the contents rapidly until the liquid has reduced to 225 ml (8 fl oz). Strain, reserving the juices.
4. Mix the minced chicken and juices together, then check the seasoning. Pack into small dishes, cover with clingfilm and chill in the refrigerator for at least 4 hours.
5. Leave at cool room temperature for 30 minutes before serving. Garnish with fresh tarragon sprigs.

COCK-A-LEEKIE SOUP

SERVES 4-6

15 g (½ oz) butter
275 g-335 g (10-12 oz) chicken (1 large or 2 small
  chicken portions)
335 g (12 oz) leeks, trimmed and washed
1.2 lt (2 pt) chicken stock
1 bouquet garni
salt and pepper
6 prunes, stoned and halved
fresh parsley sprigs, to garnish

1. Melt the butter in a large saucepan and fry
the chicken quickly until golden on all sides.
2. Cut the white part of the leeks into four
lengthways and chop into 5 cm (2 in) pieces,
reserving the green parts, Wash well. Add the
white parts to the pan and fry for 5 minutes,
until soft.
3. Add the stock and bouquet garni and season
to taste. Bring to the boil and simmer for
30 minutes or until the chicken is tender.
Shred the reserved green parts of the leeks,
then add to the pan with the prunes. Simmer
for a further 30 minutes.
4. To serve, remove the chicken, then cut the
meat into large pieces, discarding the skin and
bones. Put the meat in a warmed tureen and
pour over the soup. Serve hot, garnished with
parsley sprigs.

VARIATION Add a small quantity of leftover
joint or uncooked beef to the dish. Cooked
beef should be added towards the end of the
cooking time to prevent it becoming tough.

CLEAR CHICKEN AND MUSHROOM SOUP

SERVES 4

2 chicken legs, about 450 g (1 lb) total weight
2 × 15 ml tbs oil
175 g (6 oz) onion, peeled and thinly sliced
5 cm (2 in) piece of fresh root ginger, peeled
  and finely chopped
50 g (2 oz) long-grain brown rice
1 × 15 ml tbs soy sauce
salt and pepper
115 g (4 oz) button mushrooms, wiped and sliced
6 salad onions, cut into fine shreds
4 × 15 ml tbs sherry
dash of Worcester sauce

1. Skin the chicken and halve each portion.
Heat the oil in a large saucepan, add the onion
and fry until lightly brown. Stir in the ginger
and rice and fry for about 30 seconds.
2. Pour in 1.8 lt (3 pt) water with the soy sauce
and bring to the boil. Add the chicken and
seasoning. Cover and simmer for 30 minutes or
until the chicken and rice are tender.
3. Take the chicken out of the pan and shred
the flesh. Return to the pan with mushrooms,
salad onions, sherry and Worcester sauce.
Simmer for about 5 minutes. Adjust seasoning.

VARIATION To give this soup a more
distinctive flavour try using cup or field
mushrooms.
  Alternatively, simply sauté 1 red or green
pepper, seeded and thinly sliced, with the
onion. For the finishing touch, garnish with a
salad onion tassel. Trim the onion, discarding
the dark ends, to 8 cm (3 in) lengths. With a
sharp knife shred each end, leaving about 2 cm
(¾ in) intact in the middle. Leave in a bowl of
iced water to open out.

Cock-a-Leekie Soup

CHINESE-STYLE CHICKEN AND SWEETCORN SOUP

SERVES 2-3

600 ml (20 fl oz) chicken stock
2.5 cm (1 in) piece of fresh root ginger, peeled
    and finely chopped
1 salad onion, thinly sliced
115 g (4 oz) raw chicken, skinned
    and finely shredded
198 g can sweetcorn kernels, drained
2 × 5 ml tsp medium sherry
1 × 15 ml tbs cornflour
1 × size 3 egg white
salt and pepper

1. Boil the stock in a small pan and stir in the
ginger, onion and chicken. Simmer for 2-3
minutes, then stir in the sweetcorn and sherry.
2. Blend the cornflour with a little water. Add
to the soup and simmer until thickened.
3. Beat the egg white lightly with a fork, then
pour into the soup and cook for 1-2 minutes.
Stir well and adjust seasoning before serving.

CURRIED CHICKEN SOUP

SERVES 4

1 onion, skinned and finely chopped
115 g (4 oz) split red lentils, boiled rapidly for
    10 minutes, then drained
1 × 5 ml tsp ground turmeric
1 × 5 ml tsp garam masala
½ × 5 ml tsp chilli powder, or to taste
900 ml (1½ pt) chicken stock
225 g (8 oz) cooked chicken meat, skinned and
    coarsely chopped
salt and pepper
low-fat natural yogurt, fresh parsley sprigs, and
    paprika, to garnish

1. Bring onion, lentils, spices, stock and half
the chicken to the boil in a saucepan. Cover
and simmer for 20 minutes. Cool slightly, then
purée in a blender or food processor.
2. Return the mixture to the pan and add the
remaining chicken. Heat gently, then simmer
for a further 10 minutes. Season with salt and
pepper to taste and serve garnished with
yogurt, parsley and paprika.

TURKEY AND HAZELNUT SOUP

SERVES 4-6

75 g (3 oz) hazelnuts
15 g (½ oz) butter
1 onion, skinned and roughly chopped
½ × 5 ml tsp paprika
225 g (8 oz) turkey breast fillet,
    skinned and chopped
900 ml (1½ pt) chicken stock
1 × size 3 egg yolk
150 ml (5 fl oz) fresh single cream
1 × 15 ml tbs chopped fresh chervil
salt and pepper
fresh chervil sprigs, to garnish

1. Toast the hazelnuts on a sheet of foil under
the grill, turning frequently. Put in a blender or
food processor and finely chop.
2. Melt the butter in a saucepan, add the onion
and paprika, cover and cook for 5 minutes,
until soft. Add the turkey breast and stock and
simmer for 5 minutes, until tender. Do not
over-cook or the turkey will become rubbery.
3. Allow to cool slightly, then purée in a
blender or food processor. Blend the egg yolk
with the cream and add to the soup. Return
the soup to the pan and reheat without boiling,
stirring all the time.
4. Add hazelnuts, chervil and seasoning. Serve
hot, garnished with fresh chervil sprigs.

Chinese-Style Chicken and Sweetcorn Soup

ORIENTAL CHICKEN SALAD

SERVES 4

2.5 cm (1 in) piece of fresh root ginger, peeled
 and finely chopped
1 large garlic clove, skinned and crushed
200 ml (7 fl oz) orange juice
4 × 15 ml tbs lemon juice
4 × 15 ml tbs light soy sauce
4 × 15 ml tbs sherry
1 × 15 ml tbs white wine vinegar
1 × 5 ml tsp clear honey
4 chicken breast fillets, skinned, about
 450 g (1 lb) total weight
175 g (6 oz) baby sweetcorn, halved lengthways
115 g (4 oz) beansprouts
1 × 15 ml tbs sunflower oil
salt and pepper
1 small head Chinese leaves, shredded
1 head radicchio lettuce, shredded
1 bunch of salad onions, trimmed and sliced
1 × 15 ml tbs sesame seeds, toasted

1. Mix together the first eight ingredients and
place in a large, shallow non-metallic dish.
2. Make three shallow cuts in each chicken
breast and place in the marinade. Cover and
chill for 3–4 hours – the longer the better.
3. Cook the sweetcorn in boiling, salted water
for about 5 minutes. Add the beansprouts to
the same pan and cook for 30 seconds. Drain
and blot dry with kitchen paper. Cool.
4. Remove the chicken from the marinade.
Heat the oil in a large non-stick pan and cook
the chicken for 10-12 minutes, turning
frequently, until cooked through. Add the
marinade to the pan and simmer to thicken
slightly. Adjust seasoning. Keep warm.
5. Mix all the salad ingredients and place on a
large serving plate. Serve the warm chicken
breast on top of the salad, using the marinade as
a dressing. Garnish with toasted sesame seeds.

Oriental Chicken Salad (left); Chicken Tacos (right)

19

Chicken Liver Salad with Pear

SERVES 8

450 g (1 lb) chicken livers, trimmed
6 × 15 ml tbs vegetable oil
1 × 15 ml tbs white wine vinegar
1 × 5 ml tsp Dijon mustard
salt and pepper
2 ripe pears
1 × 15 ml tbs lemon juice
1 × 15 ml tbs brandy
1 × 5 ml tsp sugar (optional)
endive
25 g (1 oz) hazelnuts

1. Divide the chicken livers into large bite-sized pieces. Heat 4 × 15 ml tbs oil in a large frying pan. Add half the livers and cook over a high heat until well-browned yet still pink inside – they should still feel slightly soft when lightly pressed with a spoon. Lift out of the pan and place in a bowl. Brown the remaining livers similarly and add to the bowl.
2. Strain the residual oil into a jug. Whisk in the remaining oil, the vinegar, mustard and seasoning. Pour over the livers, stirring gently to mix. Cool, cover and refrigerate until required.
3. Peel, quarter, core and cut up the pears into small pieces. Immediately mix with the lemon

Chicken Liver Salad with Pear

juice and brandy, adding sugar if necessary. Stir well, cover tightly and refrigerate until serving time. Rinse and drain the endive and dry on absorbent kitchen paper. Tear into small pieces, then refrigerate in a polythene bag. Toast the hazelnuts under the grill; cool and roughly chop.

4. About 30 minutes before serving gently stir together the liver and pears (the pears will have discoloured slightly), cover and leave at room temperature. At serving time arrange the endive on individual serving plates and top with the liver mixture. Garnish with the hazelnuts.

COOK'S TIP Chicken livers should be lightly cooked to retain flavour and moisture. Pressing them gently while they're cooking is the best method of testing – if very soft and flabby they're raw; firm on the outside, yet soft inside, they're about right; very firm and they're over-cooked.

WARM VEGETABLE SALAD

SERVES 2

50 g (2 oz) carrots, peeled and cut into thin batons
2 courgettes, trimmed and sliced
50 g (2 oz) bobby or French beans, cut into
   2.5 cm (1 in) lengths
50 g (2 oz) mangetout
50 g (2 oz) broccoli florets
1½ × 5 ml tsp Dijon mustard
1 × 15 ml tbs lemon juice
3 × 15 ml tbs low-fat mayonnaise
salt and pepper
115 g (4 oz) cold cooked chicken (skinless)
chives, to garnish (optional)

1. Cook all the vegetables in boiling salted water for 2-3 minutes. Drain.
2. Stir the mustard and lemon juice into the mayonnaise, seasoning well, then mix with the drained vegetables. Spoon onto individual serving plates.
3. Place strips of cold chicken on top of the vegetables and serve immediately, garnished with chives if wished.

SPICED DUCKLING AND ORANGE SALAD

SERVES 4

1.8 kg (4 lb) oven-ready duckling
2 medium oranges
salt and pepper
3 × 15 ml tbs vegetable oil
1 × 15 ml tbs white wine vinegar
2 × 15 ml tbs low-fat mayonnaise
2 × 5 ml tsp curry powder
2 × 15 ml tbs orange marmalade
snipped fresh chives or chopped fresh parsley,
   to garnish

1. Wipe the duckling and prick well all over with a fork. Using a potato peeler or sharp knife, pare the rind from one orange and put it inside the duckling. Place the duckling on a rack or trivet in a roasting tin. Sprinkle with salt and pepper inside and out, then roast in the oven at 180°C/350°F/Gas Mark 4 for about 2 hours, or until the juices run clear. While still warm, strip the breast skin off the duck and reserve. Carve off all the meat and shred finely.
2. In a large bowl, mix the oil, vinegar, mayonnaise, curry powder and marmalade and season with salt and pepper. Stir in the meat.
3. Using a serrated knife, remove all the peel and pith from the oranges and divide into segments, discarding the pips and as much of the membrane as possible. Add to the duck, then cover and refrigerate.
4. Cut the reserved duck skin into strips and grill until crisp. Just before serving, sprinkle them over the salad. Top with the chives or parsley.

Chicken and Gruyère Salad

SERVES 4-6

1.1 kg (2½ lb) cooked, boned chicken, skinned
and cut into large, bite-size pieces
4 celery sticks, trimmed and thickly sliced
115 g (4 oz) Gruyère or Emmenthal cheese,
coarsely grated
2 firm, red apples, cored and roughly chopped
175 g (6 oz) seedless black grapes, halved
200 ml (7 fl oz) oil
2 × 15 ml tbs white wine vinegar
4 × 15 ml tbs soured cream
4 × 15 ml tbs low-fat mayonnaise
4 × 15 ml tbs chopped fresh parsley
75 g (3 oz) pecan nuts or walnuts, toasted
salt and pepper

1. Place the chicken, celery, cheese, apple and
grapes in a large bowl. Mix together all the
other ingredients, add to the bowl and toss well.
2. Cover and refrigerate for at least 10–15
minutes before serving.

Chicken and Grape Salad

SERVES 4-6

1.4 kg (3 lb) chicken
1 onion, skinned
1 carrot
1 bay leaf
6 peppercorns
2 × size 3 eggs
6 × 15 ml tbs lemon juice
3 × 15 ml tbs clear honey
150 ml (5 fl oz) whipping cream
225 g (8 oz) green seedless grapes, halved
50 g (2 oz) seedless raisins
salt and pepper
lettuce, shredded, and paprika, to garnish

1. Put the chicken in a large saucepan with the
onion, carrot, bay leaf and peppercorns. Cover
with water and poach for about 50 minutes or
until tender. Leave to cool in the stock.
2. Remove the chicken from the stock and cut
all the meat off the bones, discarding the skin.
Cut the meat into bite-size pieces.
3. Beat the eggs with 4 × 15 ml tbs of the
lemon juice and the honey. Put in the top of a
double saucepan or in a heatproof bowl over a
pan of hot water and heat gently, stirring, until
thick. Cover and leave to cool.
4. Whip the cream until just stiff and fold into the
cold lemon mixture. Add the remaining lemon
juice to the grapes, then combine with the
chicken, raisins, sauce and seasoning. Pile onto a
serving plate; garnish with lettuce and paprika.

Chicken and Cheese Salad

SERVES 4

250 g (9 oz) boneless cooked chicken, sliced
75 g (3 oz) brown rice, cooked
115 g (4 oz) Blue Cheshire cheese, cubed
50 g (2 oz) radishes, trimmed and sliced
25 g (1 oz) sultanas
2 celery sticks, sliced
1 Cox's eating apple, cored and diced
1 × 15 ml tbs lemon juice
150 ml (5 fl oz) low-fat natural yogurt
2 × 15 ml tbs low-fat mayonnaise
fresh watercress sprigs and red apple slices,
to garnish

1. Mix the chicken, rice, cheese, radishes,
sultanas and celery together in a large bowl.
2. Coat the apple in lemon juice, then add to
the salad.
3. Mix the yogurt and mayonnaise and pour it
over the salad. Cover and chill. Serve in a large
bowl, garnished with watercress and apple slices.

Chicken and Cheese Salad

CHICKEN WITH CURRIED LEMON MAYONNAISE

SERVES 4

1.4 kg (3 lb) chicken
150 ml (5 fl oz) dry white wine
1 strip of lemon rind
1 bouquet garni
6 black peppercorns
salt and pepper
15 g (½ oz) butter or margarine
1 small onion, skinned and chopped
1 × 15 ml tbs curry powder
2 celery sticks, finely chopped
175 ml (6 fl oz) thick, low-fat mayonnaise
2 × 15 ml tbs apricot jam
finely grated rind and juice of 1 lemon
1 red or green pepper, cored, seeded and diced
2 red-skinned eating apples
150 ml (5 fl oz) double or whipping cream
lettuce, to serve

1. Put the chicken in a deep saucepan with the wine, enough water to just cover the bird, lemon rind, bouquet garni, peppercorns and a good pinch of salt. Cover and simmer for 1–1¼ hours until the chicken is tender, then leave for about 2 hours to cool in the liquid.
2. Remove the chicken from the liquid; strain the liquid into a saucepan, then boil until reduced to a few tablespoons. Cool for 5 minutes.
3. Meanwhile, remove the chicken from the bones and dice the meat, discarding all skin.
4. Melt the fat in a small pan, add the onion and curry powder and fry until soft. Add the celery and fry for 2 minutes, stirring. Cool for 10 minutes.
5. Add the onion and celery to the mayonnaise with the apricot jam, grated lemon rind and juice and the diced pepper. Thin with the reduced cooking liquid. Taste and adjust seasoning.
6. Core and dice or slice the apples, but do not peel them. Whip the cream until thick, then fold into the mayonnaise with the apples and chicken. Pile into a salad bowl lined with lettuce leaves. Chill for about 30 minutes before serving.

CHICKEN AND AVOCADO SALAD

SERVES 4-6

1.1 kg (2½ lb) cooked chicken
9 × 15 ml tbs olive oil
juice of 1 lemon
1 × 5 ml tsp bottled creamed horseradish
½ × 5 ml tsp Dijon mustard
2 ripe avocados
salt and pepper
fresh coriander sprigs and lemon slices,
    to garnish

1. Remove all the meat from the chicken carcass, taking care to cut thin, even slices which will look attractive in the finished dish.
2. To make the dressing, whisk together the oil, lemon juice, horseradish and mustard in a large bowl. Coat the chicken in the dressing, then cover and leave for 30 minutes to 1 hour.
3. Halve the avocados and remove the stones. Peel off the skin, then cut the flesh lengthways into thin, even slices. Arrange the chicken and avocado slices alternately on a flat, round or oval plate, overlapping them slightly. Chop any remaining oddly shaped pieces of chicken and avocado and toss them together. Pile this mixture into the centre of the plate.
4. Season the dressing remaining in the bowl and brush it over the avocado slices to prevent discoloration. Garnish the salad with fresh coriander and lemon slices, and serve immediately with the dressing served separately.

Chicken and Avocado Salad

25

CHICKEN AND COURGETTE PITTA POCKETS

SERVES 4

6 × 15 ml tbs low-fat natural yogurt
2 × 15 ml tbs wholegrain mustard
juice of 1 large lime
salt and pepper
450 g (1 lb) chicken fillet (skinless)
225 g (8 oz) small courgettes, trimmed and sliced
4 small pitta breads
2 eating apples, sliced
salad leaves, shredded, to garnish

1. Mix together the yogurt, mustard, lime juice and seasoning. Dice the chicken and stir into the marinade. Cover and leave to stand for about 10 minutes, longer if possible.
2. Place the chicken and the marinade in a foil-lined grill pan and grill for about 12 minutes, turning occasionally, until cooked through.
3. Meanwhile, blanch the courgettes in boiling salted water for 1 minute; drain.
4. Halve each pitta, open out and fill with a mixture of chicken, courgettes and apple slices and serve with salad leaves.

SESAME CHICKEN PITTAS

SERVES 4

2 × 15 ml tbs sesame oil
1 onion, skinned and sliced
115 g (4 oz) broccoli, cut into tiny florets
1 red pepper, cored, seeded and diced
225 g (8 oz) cooked chicken, sliced into thin strips
115 g (4 oz) beansprouts
1 × 15 ml tbs dark soy sauce
2 × 15 ml tbs sesame seeds, toasted
4 large pitta breads

1. Heat the oil in a large frying pan, add the onion and stir-fry for 2 minutes. Add the broccoli and pepper and cook for 3-4 minutes, stirring frequently.
2. Add the chicken strips to the pan, stir well, then add the beansprouts and soy sauce. Continue to cook for 2-3 minutes. Sprinkle the sesame seeds over and stir to combine. Remove from the heat and keep warm.
3. Cut through a long side of each pitta bread and open the cavity to form a pocket. Place the pitta breads on a baking tray in the oven at 200°C/400°F/Gas Mark 6 for 5 minutes.
4. Using a slotted spoon, fill each pitta pocket with the chicken mixture. Serve immediately.

CROSTINI

SERVES 4

2 × 15 ml tbs olive oil
225 g (8 oz) chicken livers, trimmed and
   cut into bite-sized pieces
1 small onion, skinned and finely chopped
1 garlic clove, skinned and crushed
2 celery sticks, finely chopped
2 × 5 ml tsp tomato purée
2 × 5 ml tsp chopped sage or parsley
salt and pepper
about 4 × 15 ml tbs dry white wine
toasted French bread, to serve
sage leaves, to garnish

1. Heat the oil in a frying pan, add the chicken livers and fry briskly until just changing colour, stirring constantly. Remove and set aside.
2. Add the onion, garlic and celery to the pan and fry gently for 7-10 minutes until softened. Stir in the tomato purée, sage and seasoning.
3. Return the chicken livers to the pan and add enough wine to moisten. Cook gently for about 5 minutes, stirring frequently.
4. Serve on French bread garnished with sage.

Sesame Chicken Pittas

CHICKEN TACOS

SERVES 6

6 taco shells
25 g (1 oz) butter or margarine
1 onion, peeled and chopped
450 g (1 lb) cooked chicken meat, diced
4 tomatoes, skinned and chopped
salt and pepper
½ lettuce, shredded
115 g (4 oz) Cheddar cheese, grated
Tabasco sauce, to taste

1. Put the taco shells in the oven at 150°C/300°F/Gas Mark 2 for 2–3 minutes to warm, or according to the packet instructions.
2. To make the filling, melt the butter or margarine in a frying pan, add the onion and fry for about 5 minutes or until soft but not coloured. Stir in the chicken and half the tomatoes, season to taste and heat through.
3. Spoon 1–2 × 15 ml tbs filling into each shell. Add a little lettuce, the remaining tomatoes and the cheese, with a few drops of Tabasco sauce. Serve immediately.

VARIATION This mixture also makes a good filling for pancakes or a tasty sauce for serving with pasta.

To add fibre to this recipe simply mix in a large can of red kidney beans with the chicken. To give this recipe a 'kick' add 1–2 × 5 ml tsp chilli powder and fry off with the onion. Take care when adding chilli powder because strengths vary from one brand to another. Always add the smallest amount, then taste before adding more. If you prefer a mild chilli flavour, buy chilli seasoning, which is a blend of chilli powder and other spices; it has less fire than real chilli powder and can be used in larger amounts.

CHICKEN EGGAH

SERVES 4–6

8 chicken thighs
600 ml (20 fl oz) chicken stock
2 × 5 ml tsp ground cumin
¼ × 5 ml tsp chilli powder
salt and pepper
115 g (4 oz) Chinese egg noodles
6 × size 3 eggs
50 g (2 oz) butter or margarine
1 onion, peeled and sliced
1 garlic clove, skinned and crushed
2 × 5 ml tsp paprika

1. Put the chicken thighs in a large saucepan, then add the stock, cumin and chilli powder and season with salt and pepper. Simmer for 30 minutes or until the chicken is tender.
2. Remove the chicken from the pan and set aside. Add 1.2 lt (2 pt) water to the pan and bring to the boil. Add the egg noodles and boil for about 5 minutes, or according to the packet instructions, until tender. Drain thoroughly in a colander or sieve.
3. Remove the chicken flesh from the bones and discard the skin. Cut the meat into small strips. Using kitchen scissors, cut the cooked, drained egg noodles into short lengths.
4. Beat the eggs lightly in a large bowl, then add the noodles and chicken and stir gently to mix. Melt the butter or margarine in a large, heavy-based frying pan, add the onion, garlic and paprika and fry gently for about 5 minutes.
5. Pour in the egg mixture and stir lightly with a fork. Cook over a moderate heat for 15 minutes or until set and golden brown underneath. Turn the eggah out on to a plate, then slide back into the pan so that the underside is uppermost. Cook for a further 15 minutes or until golden brown. Serve hot.

Chicken Eggah

POT-ROASTED CHICKEN

SERVES 6

115 g (4 oz) long-grain rice
salt and freshly ground black pepper
50 g (2 oz) raisins
2 celery sticks, finely chopped
25 g (1 oz) butter
1.8-2.3 kg (4-5 lb) chicken, without giblets
225 g (8 oz) button onions, skinned
450 g (1 lb) small tomatoes, skinned
450 g (1 lb) carrots, peeled and quartered, or
    small carrots, scraped
4 × 15 ml tbs white wine
fresh herbs, to garnish

1. Cook the rice in boiling salted water until
tender – about 20 minutes. Drain well. Stir in
the raisins, celery and butter while the rice is
still warm. Season well and allow the mixture
to cool.
2. Rinse the chicken, flushing the body cavity
under cold running water. Drain well, then pat
the bird dry on absorbent kitchen paper. Cut
off any lumps of fat.
3. Loosely spoon the rice mixture into the
body cavity of the chicken, then truss the bird
neatly, tying the leg ends together and the
wings close to the body.
4. Put the onions, tomatoes and carrots in a
medium oval casserole and pour in the wine;
season. Then place the chicken on top of the
vegetables and season the bird.
5. Cover the casserole and cook the chicken at
180°C/350°F/Gas Mark 4 for 2½ hours, or
until it is cooked through. Serve the chicken
with the vegetables and ladle some of the
cooking juices over each portion. Garnish with
fresh herbs.

Pot-Roasted Chicken

Chicken and Broccoli Hotpot

SERVES 4

450 g (1 lb) skinless chicken fillet
1 × 15 ml tbs oil
30 g packet of onion sauce mix
600 ml (20 fl oz) skimmed milk
1 × 15 ml tbs wholegrain mustard
salt and pepper
225 g (8 oz) broccoli florets
115 g (4 oz) button mushrooms, halved if large
mixed-grain rice and salad, to accompany

1. Cut the chicken into bite-size pieces and brown quickly in hot oil in a flameproof casserole. Drain on kitchen paper.
2. Make the sauce according to packet instructions, using the skimmed milk. Whisk in the wholegrain mustard; season well.
3. Layer all the ingredients into the casserole and pour over the onion sauce. Bring to the boil, cover and bake at 180°C/350°F/Gas Mark 4 for about 30 minutes, or until tender. Serve with mixed-grain rice and a crisp green salad.

Stoved Chicken

SERVES 4

25 g (1 oz) butter
1 × 15 ml tbs vegetable oil
4 chicken quarters, halved
115 g (4 oz) lean back bacon, rinded and chopped
1.1 kg (2½ lb) floury potatoes, such as King
    Edwards, peeled and cut into 0.5 cm (¼ in) slices
2 large onions, skinned and sliced
salt and pepper
2 × 5 ml tsp chopped fresh thyme or ½ × 5 ml tsp
    dried thyme
600 ml (20 fl oz) chicken stock
fresh chives, to garnish

1. Heat half the butter and the oil in a large frying pan and fry the chicken and bacon for 5 minutes, until lightly browned.
2. Place a thick layer of potato slices, then onion slices, in the base of a large ovenproof casserole. Season well, add the thyme and dot with half the remaining butter.
3. Add the chicken and bacon, seasoning to taste. Cover with the remaining onions and finally a layer of potatoes. Season and dot with the remaining butter. Pour over the stock.
4. Cover and bake at 150°C/300°F/Gas Mark 2 for about 2 hours, until the chicken is tender and the potatoes are cooked, adding a little more hot stock if necessary. Sprinkle with snipped chives just before serving.

Stuffed Roast Chicken with Prunes

SERVES 6

1.8 kg (4 lb) chicken, with giblets
225 g (8 oz) sausagemeat
450 g (1 lb) tenderised prunes
25 g (1 oz) raisins
2 slices of white bread, crusts removed
a little milk
salt and pepper
¼ × 5 ml tsp grated nutmeg
25 g (1 oz) butter
2 × 5 ml tsp cornflour, blended with
    2 × 15 ml tbs water

1. Reserving the chicken liver and heart, finely chop the giblets and mix them with the sausagemeat. Finely chop a quarter of the prunes, then add them to the sausagemeat with the raisins. Soak the bread in a little milk for 5 minutes, then squeeze it dry and add it to the sausagemeat. Season the mixture, add the nutmeg and mix well.
2. Rinse the chicken and pat dry. Loosely

Stoved Chicken

spoon the sausagemeat stuffing into the neck end of the chicken, then truss the bird neatly.
3. Heat the butter in a large oval cocotte and brown the chicken all over. Remove the cocotte from the heat and season the chicken. Cover and cook at 160°C/325°F/Gas Mark 3 for 3 hours. After 2 hours, add the remaining prunes to the liquid in the cocotte. Remove

the lid for the last 30 minutes of cooking to brown the chicken.
4. Lift out the chicken and keep hot in a serving dish. Add 150 ml (5 fl oz) water to the cooking liquor. Transfer the cocotte to the hob and thicken the sauce with the blended cornflour. Pour the sauce over the chicken and serve immediately.

33

CHICKEN WITH OYSTER SAUCE

SERVES 4

6 × 15 ml tbs oil
450 g (1 lb) skinless chicken breast fillets,
    cut into bite-size pieces
3 × 15 ml tbs oyster sauce
1 × 15 ml tbs dark soy sauce
115 ml (4 fl oz) chicken stock
2 × 5 ml tsp lemon juice
1 garlic clove, skinned and finely sliced
6-8 large flat mushrooms, about 250 g (9 oz)
    total weight, sliced
115 g (4 oz) mangetout
1 × 5 ml tsp cornflour
1 × 15 ml tbs sesame oil
salt and pepper

1. Heat 3 × 15 ml tbs oil in a wok or frying pan. Add the chicken and cook over a high heat, stirring continuously for 2–3 minutes, until lightly browned. Remove with a slotted spoon and drain on absorbent kitchen paper.
2. In a bowl, mix the oyster sauce, soy sauce, chicken stock and lemon juice. Then add the chicken and stir until thoroughly combined.
3. Heat the remaining oil over a high heat and stir-fry the garlic for about 30 seconds; add mushrooms and cook for 1 minute. Add the chicken mixture, cover and simmer for 8 minutes.
4. Stir in the mangetout and cook for a further 2–3 minutes. Mix the cornflour with 1 × 15 ml tbs water. Remove the wok or frying pan from the heat and stir in the cornflour mixture. Return to the heat, add the sesame oil and stir until the sauce has thickened. Adjust seasoning and serve.

CHICKEN WITH STEAMED VEGETABLES

SERVES 6

50 g (2 oz) butter
1 × 15 ml tbs oil
6 chicken breasts with skin and bone, about
    1.4 kg (3 lb) total weight
2 salad onions, trimmed and finely chopped
300 ml (10 fl oz) chicken stock
150 ml (5 fl oz) double cream
675 g (1½ lb) mixed vegetables, such as baby
    turnips, carrots, cauliflower, broad beans, peas,
    prepared and cut into bite-size pieces
1 × 15 ml tbs roughly chopped fresh tarragon
salt and pepper

1. Heat butter and oil in a large sauté pan and brown the chicken breasts, a few at a time. Remove chicken with a slotted spoon. Add the onion and cook, stirring, for 2–3 minutes until golden. Return the chicken to the pan with the stock.
2. Bring to the boil, cover and simmer very gently for 25–30 minutes or until the chicken is tender and cooked through. Remove to a heated serving dish. Cover and keep warm.
3. Add the cream to the cooking liquor and bring to the boil. Bubble for 4–5 minutes or until reduced by half and lightly thickened.
4. Meanwhile place the prepared vegetables in a steamer basket or colander over a pan of boiling water. Cover and steam for 4–5 minutes or until just tender.
5. Stir the tarragon and seasoning into the thickened sauce. Spoon over the chicken. Serve with the vegetables.

Chicken with Oyster Sauce

CHICKEN AND GORGONZOLA PARCELS

SERVES 4

4 skinless chicken breast fillets, about 675 g (1½ lb)
   total weight
2 × 5 ml tsp olive paste or finely chopped, black
   stoned olives
115 g (4 oz) Gorgonzola cheese (or Dolcelatte,
   Blue Brie or Stilton), sliced
12 fresh sage leaves
4 slices of Parma ham or prosciutto crudo
25 g (1 oz) butter
75 g (3 oz) shallots, finely chopped
150 ml (5 fl oz) dry vermouth or white wine
salt and pepper

1. Starting at the thick side, cut a deep horizontal pocket in each chicken breast. Spread a little olive paste inside each pocket, then stuff with a quarter of the sliced cheese.
2. Lay three sage leaves on top of each breast; then wrap in a slice of Parma ham. Tie with fine string.
3. Heat the butter in a sauté pan or heavy frying pan and cook the shallots for 5 minutes or until beginning to soften. Place the chicken on top of the shallots and pour in the vermouth or wine. Bring to the boil, cover, and simmer for about 20 minutes or until the chicken is tender and cooked through. Season the sauce to taste.
4. Remove the string from the chicken. Serve immediately with a little sauce poured over, accompanied by crisp green vegetables and new potatoes.

COOK'S TIP Keep the cost down by wrapping the chicken in rindless streaky bacon instead of Parma ham.

Chicken and Gorgonzola Parcels

TURKEY ROLLS WITH SWEDE AND ORANGE

SERVES 4

115 g (4 oz) onion, skinned and finely chopped
vegetable oil
50 g (2 oz) hazelnuts, roughly chopped
50 g (2 oz) breadcrumbs
4-5 × 15 ml tbs chopped fresh parsley
grated rind and juice of 1 large orange
salt and pepper
4 turkey escalopes, each weighing 335 g (12 oz)
1 × 15 ml tbs seasoned flour
25 g (1 oz) butter or margarine
335 g (12 oz) potato, peeled and thinly sliced
335 g (12 oz) swede, peeled and thinly sliced
425 ml (15 fl oz) stock
orange slices, to garnish

1. To make the stuffing, fry the onion in 3 × 15 ml tbs oil until beginning to soften. Add the nuts and stir over a high heat until golden. Take off the heat and mix with breadcrumbs, 3 × 15 ml tbs parsley, grated orange rind and 2 × 15 ml tbs juice and seasoning. Spoon into a bowl; cool.
2. Place the turkey escalopes between sheets of clingfilm then bat out thinly. Divide the stuffing between the fillets; roll up to enclose the stuffing and tie with fine string.
3. Dip the fillets in seasoned flour then brown in 2 × 15 ml tbs oil and the fat in a large, shallow, flameproof casserole. Remove from the pan and pour off all but 1 × 15 ml tbs fat.
4. Add the potato and swede and stir over the heat until beginning to brown. Replace the turkey, adding the stock, 3 × 15 ml tbs orange juice and seasoning. Bring to the boil.
5. Cover the dish tightly and simmer for about 30 minutes, or until the meat and vegetables are tender. Remove turkey, keep warm. Reduce liquid by boiling. Adjust seasoning to serve; garnish with parsley and orange slices.

Chicken Drumsticks with Watercress Sauce

SERVES 8

12 plump chicken drumsticks, about 1.4 kg (3 lb)
  total weight
25 g (1 oz) polyunsaturated margarine
115 g (4 oz) chicken livers
225 g (8 oz) onion, skinned and roughly chopped
75 g (3 oz) coarse oatmeal, toasted
1 large bunch watercress
1 × 15 ml tbs lemon juice
½ × size 3 egg, beaten
 salt and pepper
1 × 15 ml tbs seasoned flour
3 × 15 ml tbs polyunsaturated oil
450 ml (16 fl oz) chicken stock
2 × 15 ml tbs low-fat soft cheese

1. Pull the skin off each drumstick. Carefully split down one side and fillet out the bone; snip away any coarse sinews.
2. Heat the margarine in a frying pan; add the livers and half the onion. Fry over a moderate heat for a few minutes until the livers are just cooked. Lift the livers out of the pan, using a slotted spoon, then chop roughly. Place in a bowl, adding the fat and onion from the pan; stir in the toasted oatmeal; cool.
3. Rinse and drain the watercress. Pat dry with kitchen paper, then finely chop half and roughly chop the remainder. Stir the finely chopped portion into the livers with the lemon juice, egg and seasoning. Spoon the stuffing into the boned chicken and sew up each drumstick using fine string.
4. Dip the chicken into seasoned flour. Heat the oil in a large, ovenproof casserole. Add the chicken, brown well and remove from the pan. Stir in the remaining watercress and onion. Fry for 1-2 minutes, then pour in the stock. Bring to the boil, season and replace the chicken.
5. Cover tightly and simmer for 25-30 minutes,

or until tender. Lift out the chicken and ease off the string. Thickly slice each drumstick; place in a serving dish. Cover and keep warm.
6. Purée the pan ingredients until smooth. Reheat gently and whisk in the cheese. Adjust seasoning and spoon over the chicken.

Chicken with Coconut and Coriander

SERVES 4

50 g (2 oz) creamed coconut
1 garlic clove, skinned and crushed
2 × 15 ml tbs lemon juice
1 × 15 ml tbs vegetable oil
2 × 5 ml tsp each ground coriander and cumin
salt and pepper
8 boneless chicken thighs, about 565 g (1¼ lb)
  total weight
4 × 15 ml tbs chopped fresh coriander
1 bunch salad onions, trimmed and finely chopped,
  reserving green tops
slices of lemon and lime
mixed long-grain, white and wild rice, to
  accompany

1. Chop the coconut and dissolve in 200 ml (7 fl oz) boiling water. Mix in the crushed garlic, lemon juice, oil, spices and seasoning. Cool.
2. Open up the chicken thighs and stuff with half the fresh coriander, the chopped onions and seasoning. Reshape. Thread one or two thighs onto a wooden skewer with a slice of lemon and lime. Place in a shallow non-metallic dish. Pour the coconut mixture over them, cover and marinate in the refrigerator overnight.
3. Place the chicken in a grill pan, spoon over most of the juices. Grill for about 20 minutes, basting with the remaining marinade.
4. Stir the remaining coriander, snipped onion tops and plenty of seasoning through the cooked rice to serve with the chicken.

SHREDDED CHICKEN WITH MUSHROOMS AND WALNUTS

SERVES 4

4 chicken breast fillets, each weighing about
   115 g (4 oz), skinned and cut into thin strips
5 cm (2 in) piece of fresh root ginger, peeled
   and thinly sliced
3 × 15 ml tbs soy sauce
4 × 15 ml tbs dry sherry
1 × 5 ml tsp five spice powder
3 × 15 ml tbs vegetable oil
115 g (4 oz) mushrooms, halved
¼ cucumber, cut into chunks
75 g (3 oz) walnut pieces, roughly chopped
pepper

1. Put the chicken in a bowl with the ginger, soy sauce, sherry and five spice powder. Stir well to mix, then cover and leave to marinate for at least 1 hour.
2. Remove the chicken from the marinade with a slotted spoon, reserving the marinade.
3. Heat the oil in a large frying pan or wok. Add the chicken and cook for 3-4 minutes, stirring continuously.
4. Add the mushrooms, cucumber and walnuts and continue to cook for 1-2 minutes, until the chicken is cooked and the vegetables are tender but still crisp.
5. Stir in the reserved marinade and cook for 1 minute, until hot. Season to taste with pepper. Serve immediately with rice or noodles.

Shredded Chicken with Mushrooms and Walnuts

GREEN FRICASSÉE OF CHICKEN

SERVES 4

2 × 15 ml tbs plain wholemeal flour
salt and pepper
4 chicken quarters, halved
15 g (½ oz) butter
1 × 15 ml tbs vegetable oil
300 ml (10 fl oz) dry white wine
900 g (2 lb) spinach, trimmed
1 × 15 ml tbs cornflour
150 ml (5 fl oz) fresh double cream
3 × 15 ml tbs chopped fresh parsley
freshly grated nutmeg

1. Season the flour, then use to coat the chicken. Heat the butter and oil in a large frying pan and fry the chicken until browned. Pour in the wine, cover and simmer for 20-30 minutes or until the chicken is tender.
2. Meanwhile, wash the spinach, then put into a large saucepan with just the water clinging to the leaves. Cover with a tight lid and cook for 5 minutes or until the spinach is tender. Drain, then transfer to a large casserole.
3. Arrange the chicken on top of the spinach, reserving the wine juices. Cover and bake at 160°C/325°F/Gas Mark 3 for 20 minutes.
4. When ready to serve, blend the cornflour with a little of the reserved juices. Heat the

Turkey Escalopes with Damsons

40

wine juices in the pan, then stir in the cream and cornflour mixture. Bring to the boil, then simmer, stirring constantly until thick. Stir in the parsley and season to taste with salt, pepper and nutmeg. Pour the sauce over the chicken and serve immediately with rice, noodles or baked potatoes.

TURKEY ESCALOPES WITH DAMSONS

SERVES 4

2 turkey breast fillets, each weighing about
   225 g (8 oz), skinned and cut widthways into
   5 cm (2 in) slices
75 ml (3 fl oz) unsweetened apple juice
3 × 15 ml tbs soy sauce
3 × 15 ml tbs dry sherry
I small garlic clove, skinned and crushed
I × 5 ml tsp chopped fresh thyme or ¼ × 5 ml tsp
   dried thyme
15 g (½ oz) butter
I × 15 ml tbs vegetable oil
225 g (8 oz) damsons or plums, halved and stoned
pepper

I. Pound the turkey slices with a rolling pin or meat mallet until they are about 2.5 cm (1 in) thick. Place in a large shallow dish and pour over the apple juice, soy sauce, sherry, garlic and thyme. Cover and leave in the refrigerator to marinate for 3-4 hours or overnight.
2. Remove the turkey, reserving the marinade. Heat the butter and oil in a large frying pan and quickly fry the turkey until browned on both sides. Add the damsons or plums, reserved marinade and pepper to taste.
3. Cover and simmer gently for 10-15 minutes, until cooked and tender, stirring occasionally. Serve with green beans and boiled potatoes.

LEMON AND LIME STIR-FRIED CHICKEN

SERVES 8

2 × 15 ml tbs walnut oil
2 × 15 ml tbs olive oil
6 × 15 ml tbs each fresh lime and lemon juice
2 garlic cloves, skinned and crushed
salt and pepper
1.1 kg (2½ lb) chicken breast fillets, skinned and
   cut into thin strips
2 bunches of salad onions, trimmed and sliced
335 g (12 oz) mangetout, trimmed
4 × 15 ml tbs vegetable oil
115 g (4 oz) shelled pecan nuts or walnuts

I. Whisk together the oils, lime and lemon juice, garlic and seasoning in a medium bowl. Add the chicken and salad onions to the marinade, cover and leave to marinate in the refrigerator for at least 4 hours.
2. Blanch the mangetout in boiling salted water for 1 minute only. Drain and rinse in cold water.
3. Heat the vegetable oil in a large wok or frying pan. Drain the chicken from the marinade, reserving the juices. Add the chicken and nuts to the pan and stir-fry over a high heat for a few minutes or until the chicken is golden brown and tender.
4. Add the mangetout to the pan with the reserved marinade juices and bubble for 1-2 minutes or until piping hot. Adjust seasoning and serve immediately.

CHICKEN PUFF PIE

SERVES 4-6

900 g (2 lb) chicken
I bay leaf
2 sprigs of fresh rosemary or marjoram
  or 2 × 5 ml tsp dried
salt and pepper
4 leeks, trimmed, washed and cut into
  2 cm (¾ in) lengths
2 large carrots, peeled and thickly sliced
115 g (4 oz) boiled ham, cut into bite-size pieces
25 g (I oz) butter or margarine
I onion, skinned and chopped
3 × 15 ml tbs flour
150 ml (5 fl oz) milk
4 × 15 ml tbs double cream
213 g chilled puff pastry
I × size 3 egg, beaten, to glaze

1. Put the chicken in a large saucepan with the herbs and salt and pepper to taste. Cover with water and bring to the boil, then cover and simmer for 45-60 minutes until tender.
2. Remove the chicken from the liquid and leave to cool. Add the leeks and carrots to the liquid, bring to the boil and simmer until just tender. Remove with a slotted spoon.
3. Take the chicken meat off the bones, discarding the skin. Cut into bite-size chunks. Mix the chicken with the ham and cooked leeks and carrots in a 1.2 lt (2 pt) pie dish.
4. Melt the fat in a clean saucepan, add the onion and fry gently until soft. Sprinkle in the flour and cook for 1-2 minutes, stirring, then gradually add 600 ml (20 fl oz) of the cooking liquid (discarding the bay leaf and herb sprigs, if used). Bring to the boil and simmer, stirring, until thick, then stir in the milk and cream, seasoning to taste. Pour into the pie dish and leave for about 30 minutes until cold.
5. Roll out the pastry on a floured work surface until about 2.5 cm (1 in) larger all round than the pie dish. Cut off a strip from all round the edge of the pastry. Place the strip on the moistened rim of the pie dish, moisten the strip, then place the pastry lid on top.
6. Press the edge firmly to seal, then knock up and flute. Make a hole in the centre of the pie and use any pastry trimmings to decorate. Brush with beaten egg, then bake in the oven at 190°C/375°F/Gas Mark 5 for 30 minutes until puffed up and golden brown. Serve hot.

VARIATIONS
● Replace the leeks with 6 celery sticks, cleaned and cut in the same way. Add them to the pan 3 minutes after adding the carrots.
● Replace the leeks with 8 Jerusalem artichokes, peeled and thickly sliced.
● Replace one of the carrots with 1 medium turnip, peeled and roughly cubed.
● Replace the carrots with 1 medium celeriac, peeled and cubed.
● Replace the puff pastry with shortcrust.
● Add 115 g (4 oz) sliced mushrooms and 1 × 5 ml tsp celery seeds when frying onion.

LEMON CHICKEN BROCHETTES WITH HERB BUTTER PASTA

SERVES 4

225 g (8 oz) fresh whole chicken livers,
  washed and trimmed
4 chicken breast fillets, cut into bite-size pieces
3 small lemons or limes, 2 thinly sliced
115 ml (4 fl oz) olive oil
I garlic clove, skinned and crushed
50 g (2 oz) onion or shallot, skinned
  and finely chopped
115 g (4 oz) butter
I × 15 ml tbs wholegrain mustard
2 × 15 ml tbs chopped fresh mixed herbs
salt and pepper
noodles, to serve
chopped fresh herbs, to garnish

Lemon Chicken Brochettes with Herb Butter Pasta

1. Thread the livers, chicken and lemon slices onto small skewers or brochettes. Place in a shallow non-metallic dish.
2. Mix together the oil, the grated rind and juice of one lemon and the garlic. Pour over the skewers, cover and marinate for 2-3 hours or overnight.
3. Beat the onion into the butter with the mustard, herbs and seasoning.

4. Cook the brochettes under a hot grill for 10-12 minutes, or until the chicken is cooked but the livers are still slightly pink in the centre. Brush with the marinade from time to time as they cook.
5. Meanwhile cook the noodles and toss immediately in the prepared herb butter. Serve the brochettes on a bed of the buttered noodles, garnished with chopped fresh herbs.

43

CHICKEN AND MUSHROOM LASAGNE

SERVES 8

1.8 kg (4 lb) oven-ready chicken
slices of carrot and onion and a bay leaf
   for flavouring
salt and pepper
oil
275 g (10 oz) lasagne
450 g (1 lb) mushrooms: button,
   flat and brown cap
175 g (6 oz) butter or margarine
2 × 15 ml tbs lemon juice
115 g (4 oz) plain white flour
1 lt (1 pt 14 fl oz) milk
150 g (5 oz) packet full-fat soft cheese with garlic
   and herbs, such as Boursin
3 × 15 ml tbs chopped fresh tarragon or
   2 × 5 ml tsp dried
2 large garlic cloves, skinned and crushed
225 g (8 oz) frozen leaf spinach, thawed, drained
   and finely chopped
75 g (3 oz) shredded Parma ham or roast ham
175 g (6 oz) Gruyère cheese, grated
50 g (2 oz) fresh white breadcrumbs
fresh herbs and lemon slices, to garnish

1. In a large saucepan, cover the chicken with cold water. Add the carrot, onion and bay leaf together with the seasoning and bring to the boil. Cover and simmer for about 1 hour, or until the chicken is thoroughly cooked. Test by inserting a skewer into the thigh; the juices should run clear.
2. Lift the chicken onto a plate and leave to cool slightly. Divide the flesh into bite–size pieces and set aside. Return the skin and bones to the saucepan of stock. Bubble down the stock until you are left with 1 lt (1 pt 14 fl oz); strain, skim away the fat and reserve the stock.
3. Meanwhile, bring a large saucepan of salted water to the boil (use two if necessary). Add a dash of oil to each, followed by the lasagne. Cook according to packet instructions, stirring occasionally. When tender, drain in a colander and immediately run cold water over the pasta: this will stop it from cooking further and rinses off some of the starch. Spread the pasta out on clean tea towels and cover with a damp tea towel until required.
4. Wipe the mushrooms; leave whole, or quarter and slice, depending on their size. Melt 50 g (2 oz) of the butter in a large saucepan. Add the mushrooms with the lemon juice and

about 1-2 minutes. Mix in the soft cheese with the tarragon, garlic and chopped spinach. Adjust the seasoning to taste.

6. Spoon a little of the sauce into the base of a 4.8 lt (8 pt) ovenproof dish or two smaller dishes. Top with a layer of pasta followed by the chicken, mushrooms and ham. Spoon over more of the sauce, then continue layering the ingredients underneath. Sprinkle over the Gruyère cheese and fresh breadcrumbs.

7. Stand the dish on a baking tray, then cook at 200°C/400°F/Gas Mark 6 for 1-1¼ hours. The lasagne should be piping hot and well browned. Garnish and serve.

CHICKEN AND PRAWN RISOTTO

SERVES 4

175 g (6 oz) chicken breast fillets, cut into
   2.5 cm (1 in) pieces
1 small onion, skinned and sliced
1 garlic clove, skinned and crushed
1 lt (1¾ pt) chicken stock
225 g (8 oz) brown rice
50 g (2 oz) small button mushrooms, wiped
pinch of ground saffron
salt and pepper
115 g (4 oz) cooked peeled prawns
50 g (2 oz) petits pois
12 whole cooked prawns, to garnish

1. Place all the ingredients, except the prawns and petits pois, in a large saucepan. Bring to the boil and simmer, uncovered, for 35 minutes, until the chicken is tender.

2. Stir in the peeled prawns and petits pois. Cook over a high heat for about 5 minutes, stirring occasionally until most of the liquid has been absorbed.

3. Adjust seasoning. Place in a warmed serving dish and garnish with the whole prawns.

Chicken and Mushroom Lasagne

seasoning. Cover and cook over a fairly high heat for about 3-4 minutes, then remove from the pan with a slotted spoon. Bubble the juices to evaporate any excess moisture until there is only butter left in the saucepan.

5. Melt the remaining butter in the same saucepan. Carefully stir in the flour and cook for 1 minute before slowly blending in the milk and the reserved chicken stock. Gradually bring to the boil, stirring all the time, and cook for

QUICK CHICKEN CURRY

SERVES 4-6

2 × 15 ml tbs vegetable oil
3 bay leaves
2 cardamom pods, crushed
1 cinnamon stick, broken into short lengths
1 onion, skinned and thinly sliced
1 green pepper, seeded and sliced (optional)
2 × 5 ml tsp paprika
1½ × 5 ml tsp garam masala
½ × 5 ml tsp turmeric
½ × 5 ml tsp chilli powder
salt and pepper
50 g (2 oz) unsalted cashew nuts
675 g (1½ lb) chicken breast fillets, skinned and
    cut into bite-size pieces
2 medium potatoes, blanched, peeled and cut into
    chunks
4 tomatoes, skinned and chopped, or
    227 g can tomatoes
mint leaves, yogurt and paprika, to garnish

1. Heat the oil in a flameproof casserole, add the bay leaves, cardamom and cinnamon and fry over moderate heat for 1–2 minutes. Add the onion and green pepper (if using), with the spices and salt and pepper to taste. Pour in enough water to moisten, then stir to mix for 1 minute.

2. Add the cashews, chicken and potatoes, cover and simmer for 10 minutes. Turn the chicken occasionally during this time to ensure even cooking.

3. Add the tomatoes and continue cooking a further 10 minutes until the chicken and potatoes are tender. Taste and adjust seasoning. Garnish with mint leaves, yogurt and a sprinkling of paprika. Serve with boiled rice.

VARIATION Use turkey fillets instead of the chicken breast fillets used here.

Quick Chicken Curry

Stir-Fried Chicken with Courgettes

SERVES 4

2 × 15 ml tbs vegetable oil
1 garlic clove, skinned and crushed
450 g (1 lb) chicken breast fillets, skinned and
   cut into thin strips
450 g (1 lb) courgettes, cut into thin strips
1 red pepper, seeded and cut into thin strips
3 × 15 ml tbs dry sherry
1 × 15 ml tbs soy sauce
4 × 15 ml tbs natural yogurt (optional)
pepper

1. Heat the oil in a large frying pan or wok, add the garlic and fry for 1 minute. Add the chicken and cook for 3-4 minutes, stirring.
2. Add the courgettes and pepper and continue frying for 1-2 minutes or until the chicken is cooked and the vegetables are just tender.
3. Stir in the sherry and soy sauce and cook for 1 minute. Stir in the yogurt, if using, and season to taste with pepper. Serve immediately.

Chicken Stroganoff

SERVES 4

1 × 15 ml tbs vegetable oil
50 g (2 oz) butter
450 g (1 lb) chicken breast fillets, sliced into
   very thin strips
2 × 15 ml tbs brandy
1 garlic clove, skinned and crushed
salt and pepper
225 g (8 oz) button mushrooms, wiped and sliced
1 green pepper, seeded and sliced
4 × 15 ml tbs soured cream

1. Heat the oil and butter in a large sauté pan and brown the chicken. Set aside. Heat the brandy in

a ladle, ignite and pour it over the chicken. Return to heat then add garlic and seasoning.
2. Cover the pan and simmer for 4-5 minutes.
3. Increase the heat, add the mushrooms and pepper and cook for 3-4 minutes, until soft.
4. Reduce the heat, stir in the soured cream, taste and adjust seasoning. Serve immediately.

VARIATION Use turkey fillets instead of chicken, if preferred.

Chinese Chicken with Vegetables

SERVES 4

450 g (1 lb) chicken meat, such as breast fillet
3 × 15 ml tbs vegetable oil
1 × 5 ml tsp salt
2 × 15 ml tbs soy sauce
2-3 celery sticks, trimmed and thinly sliced
½ green pepper, seeded and thinly sliced
410 g can beansprouts, drained
227 g can water chestnuts
50 g (2 oz) mushrooms, trimmed and halved
150 ml (5 fl oz) chicken stock
1 × 15 ml tbs cornflour
salt and pepper
50 g (2 oz) flaked almonds, toasted

1. Carefully slice the uncooked chicken into thin strips, about 0.5 cm (¼ in) wide.
2. Heat the oil in a large frying pan and add the chicken and salt. Stir-fry for 3-5 minutes. Add the soy sauce and blend well.
3. Add the celery, green pepper, beansprouts, chestnuts, mushrooms and stock. Cover and simmer for 15 minutes.
4. Blend the cornflour with a little water and add to the pan. Bring slowly to the boil, stirring. Season and sprinkle with almonds.

Stir-Fried Chicken with Courgettes

CHICKEN THIGHS WITH SPICY TOMATO SAUCE

SERVES 4

15 g (½ oz) butter
1 × 15 ml tbs vegetable oil
1 onion, skinned and chopped
1 garlic clove, skinned and crushed
1 × 5 ml tsp ground cumin
1 × 5 ml tsp ground coriander
large pinch of chilli powder
8 chicken thighs
400 g can chopped tomatoes
1 × 15 ml tbs tomato purée
salt and pepper
2 × 15 ml tbs chopped fresh parsley

1. Heat the butter and oil in a large frying pan and add the onion and garlic. Cover and cook for 4–5 minutes, until the onion is softened. Add the cumin, coriander and chilli powder and cook for 1 minute, stirring continuously.
2. Push the onions to one side of the pan, then add the chicken thighs, a few at a time, and brown on both sides. Remove the chicken. Stir in the tomatoes and the tomato purée and season to taste. Bring to the boil, stirring continuously.
3. Put back the chicken thighs, cover and simmer gently for about 30 minutes or until the chicken is tender. Stir in the parsley and serve immediately with boiled rice.

Chicken Thighs with Spicy Tomato Sauce

CHICKEN AND GRUYÈRE CRÊPES

SERVES 4-8

150 g (5 oz) plain flour
salt and pepper
1 × size 3 egg, beaten
300 ml (10 fl oz) milk
225 g (8 oz) frozen chopped spinach
335 g (12 oz) boneless cooked chicken,
    chopped into small dice
175 g (6 oz) Gruyère cheese, grated
150 ml (5 fl oz) double cream
½ × 5 ml tsp ground mace or grated nutmeg
50 g (2 oz) butter
300 ml (10 fl oz) dry white wine
oil for frying the crêpes

1. Make the batter for the crêpes. Mix 115 g (4 oz) of the flour in a bowl with a pinch of salt. Make a well in the centre and add the egg. Gradually whisk in the milk until a smooth batter is formed. Leave to stand while preparing the filling and sauce.
2. Make the filling. Put the frozen spinach in a heavy-based saucepan and heat gently until thawed, stirring frequently. Put the chicken and spinach in a bowl with 50 g (2 oz) Gruyère, 2 × 15 ml tbs cream, half the mace or nutmeg and salt and pepper to taste. Stir well to mix.
3. Make the sauce. Melt the butter in a saucepan, add the remaining flour and cook gently, stirring, for 1-2 minutes. Remove from the heat and gradually blend in the wine. Bring to the boil, stirring constantly, then add the remaining cream and simmer for 3 minutes until thick and smooth. Add 75 g (3 oz) cheese, the remaining mace and nutmeg and salt and pepper to taste. Stir until the cheese has melted, then remove from the heat.
4. Make the crêpes. Heat a little oil in a pancake pan until very hot. Whisk the batter well, then swirl one-eighth into the pan. Cook over high heat for 1-2 minutes until set and golden on the underside. Toss or turn the crêpe over and cook for a further 30 seconds, then slide it out of the pan. Repeat with the remaining batter to make 8 crêpes altogether.
5. Spoon the chicken and spinach filling onto the crêpes, dividing it equally between them. Roll or fold the crêpes up around the filling, then place seam side down in individual gratin dishes. Pour the sauce over the crêpes and sprinkle with the remaining cheese. Bake at 180°C/350°F/Gas Mark 4 for 15 minutes until golden and bubbling. Serve hot.

CLUB SANDWICHES

SERVES 2

6 rashers streaky bacon, rinded
6 slices white bread, toasted
about 3 × 15 ml tbs mayonnaise
a few lettuce leaves
2 large slices cooked chicken or turkey
salt and pepper
1 large tomato, sliced

1. Fry the bacon in its own fat until crisp; drain on absorbent kitchen paper. Spread one side of each slice of toast with some of the mayonnaise.
2. Arrange half the lettuce on two slices of toast; top with chicken or turkey. Sprinkle with salt and pepper then add another slice of toast, mayonnaise side up.
3. Arrange the rest of the lettuce, the tomato slices, and the bacon on the two sandwiches. Top with the remaining toast slices, mayonnaise side down.
4. Cut the sandwiches diagonally into quarters and secure each with a cocktail stick. Arrange, crust sides down, on two plates.

Avocado with Chicken

SERVES 4

115 g (4 oz) cooked chicken breast, chopped
1 bunch of salad onions, trimmed and chopped
2 × 15 ml tbs mayonnaise
2 × 15 ml tbs lemon juice
salt and pepper
2 small ripe avocados
grated orange rind and watercress sprigs,
    to garnish

1. Mix the chicken and salad onions with the mayonnaise, lemon juice and seasoning.
2. Halve the avocados and remove the stones. Carefully scoop out the flesh and roughly dice. Mix with the chicken and mayonnaise, then spoon back into the avocado shells.
3. Garnish with orange rind and watercress.

Chicken and Broccoli Pie

SERVES 4-6

25 g (1 oz) butter
2 carrots, peeled and diced
8 button onions, skinned
115 g (4 oz) mushrooms, wiped and trimmed
25 g (1 oz) plain wholemeal flour
450 ml (16 fl oz) milk, plus extra to glaze
450 g (1 lb) boneless cooked chicken,
    cut into strips
175 g (6 oz) broccoli, blanched
grated rind of ½ lemon
2 × 15 ml tbs fresh single cream
salt and pepper
213 g chilled puff pastry

1. Melt the butter in a large saucepan and fry the carrots, onions and mushrooms for about 8 minutes, stirring occasionally. Stir in the flour and cook for 1–2 minutes. Gradually add the milk, stirring continuously until the sauce

thickens, boils and is smooth. Simmer for 3–4 minutes.
2. Add the chicken, broccoli, lemon rind and cream to the sauce. Season to taste and pour into a 1.2 lt (2 pt) pie dish.
3. Roll out the pastry on a lightly floured surface large enough to fit the dish. Cover the pie with the pastry and moisten the edges to seal. Use any pastry trimmings to decorate. Brush with milk to glaze. Bake at 200°C/400°F/Gas Mark 6 for 25 minutes, until the pastry is golden brown. Serve at once.

VARIATION Top the pie with wholemeal shortcrust pastry instead of puff pastry.

Spiced Chicken and Chick-Pea Pot

SERVES 4

400 g can chick-pea dhal
50 g (2 oz) creamed coconut, broken up
150 ml (5 fl oz) milk
450 g (1 lb) boneless cooked chicken tikka,
    cut into bite-size pieces
2 × 15 ml tbs chopped fresh coriander
2 × 25 × 50 cm (10 × 20 in) sheets filo pastry
50 g (2 oz) butter or margarine, melted
1 × 5 ml tsp cumin seeds

1. Heat the chick-pea dhal, coconut and milk, stirring until smooth. Stir in the chicken and coriander. Spoon into a 1.3 lt (2¼ pt) pie dish.
2. Brush the filo pastry sheets with the melted butter and cut into small triangles. Lightly scrunch up the filo pastry pieces and dot over the chicken mixture to cover the surface completely. Sprinkle over the cumin seeds.
3. Bake at 200°C/400°F/Gas Mark 6 for 25–30 minutes or until golden brown and crisp.

Chicken and Broccoli Pie

CHICKEN WITH MUSHROOMS AND COGNAC

SERVES 4

25 g (I oz) butter
1.6 kg (3½ lb) chicken breasts
I clove garlic, skinned and crushed
3 × 15 ml tbs Cognac
I × 15 ml tbs plain white flour
150 ml (5 fl oz) dry white wine
450 ml (16 fl oz) chicken stock
salt and pepper
450 g (I lb) mushrooms, wiped and trimmed
150 ml carton double cream
I × 5 ml tsp cornflour
2 × 15 ml tbs green peppercorns, soaked in cold
   water overnight and drained
fresh thyme, to garnish

1. Melt the butter in a large frying pan and brown the chicken breasts. Add the garlic; brown for a further 5 minutes.
2. Lower the heat. Warm the Cognac in a ladle, set alight and pour over the chicken. Shake the pan to burn off all the alcohol. Sprinkle over the flour, then pour over the wine and stock. Season and stir well. Cover and simmer for 30 minutes.
3. Add the mushrooms to the chicken. Cook for 15 minutes or until chicken is tender.
4. Mix the cream with the cornflour. Place the chicken and vegetables in a serving dish, cover and keep warm. Mix a spoonful of cooking liquid with the cream mixture and pour into the pan. Cook gently for 5 minutes. Stir in the peppercorns. Pour the sauce over the chicken. Garnish and serve.

VARIATION Omit the peppercorns and add 335 g (12 oz) skinned shallots or baby onions with the garlic.

Chicken with Mushrooms and Cognac

55

CHICKEN WITH LEMON

SERVES 8

¼ × 5 ml tsp chilli powder
½ × 5 ml tsp garam masala
5 cm (2 in) piece of fresh root ginger,
    peeled and finely grated
2 garlic cloves, skinned and crushed
8 chicken breasts, boned and skinned
150 g (5 oz) onion, skinned and finely chopped
2 × 15 ml tbs chopped fresh coriander
grated rind and juice of 1 lemon
salt and pepper
butter
25 g (1 oz) cashew nuts
½ × 5 ml tsp saffron strands
50 g (2 oz) creamed coconut, grated
150 ml (5 fl oz) low-fat natural yogurt or
    single cream
sprigs of coriander and lemon wedges, to garnish

1. Mix together the chilli powder and half the garam masala with half the ginger and garlic.
2. Place the chicken breasts between two sheets of clingfilm or damp greaseproof paper. Pound with a rolling pin. Rub spice mixture into them, cover and marinate in the refrigerator for at least 15 minutes, preferably 1 hour.
3. Mix together 75 g (3 oz) onion, half the remaining grated ginger and 2 × 15 ml tbs chopped fresh coriander. Add the grated lemon rind, 2 × 15 ml tbs lemon juice and seasoning. Stir well until evenly blended.
4. Place the chicken breasts on a flat surface. Divide the onion mixture between them and carefully roll the breasts up around the mixture to secure the filling.
5. Rub a small roasting tin with a little butter. Add the chicken rolls and cook, uncovered, at 180°C/350°F/Gas Mark 4 for 20-25 minutes until golden and tender. The juices should run clear when tested with a skewer.
6. Place the cashew nuts, saffron and coconut in a blender or processor with 115 ml (4 fl oz)

water. Blend for 2–3 minutes.
7. Heat 25 g (1 oz) butter in a large, shallow flameproof casserole. Add the remaining chopped onions and sauté for 3-4 minutes until golden. Add remaining garam masala, grated ginger and crushed garlic and the nut liquid. Cook, stirring, for 1-2 minutes before adding the yogurt or cream.
8. Using a slotted spoon, transfer the roasted chicken breasts carefully to the yogurt sauce. Cover tightly with foil then a lid. Simmer very gently for 10-15 minutes. Adjust seasoning and garnish with coriander and lemon.

BALINESE CHICKEN

SERVES 6

115 g (4 oz) creamed coconut, chopped
6 salad onions, trimmed and finely chopped
5 cm (2 in) piece of fresh root ginger,
    peeled and finely chopped
25 g (1 oz) chopped fresh coriander
1 stalk lemon grass, finely chopped, or
    grated rind of 1 lemon
1 small red chilli, halved, seeded and
    finely chopped
4 garlic cloves, skinned and crushed
2 × 5 ml tsp ground turmeric
salt and pepper
6 chicken supremes (breast with wing) with skin,
    each weighing 225 g (8 oz), boned
olive oil
1.8 lt (3 pt) home-made chicken stock
mixture of wild and basmati rice, to serve
slivers of red chilli, to garnish

1. Over a low heat, slowly melt the coconut until it becomes a thick cream, stirring occasionally. Mix in the onions, ginger, coriander, lemon grass and chilli. Add the garlic, turmeric and seasoning. The mixture should now be a thick paste. Cool.
2. With fingertips, loosen the skin from each

Chicken with Lemon

chicken supreme to form a pocket. Work half the coconut mixture over the flesh of the six supremes and fold the skin back over to enclose. Cover and refrigerate for 1 hour.
3. Brush the chicken supremes with olive oil. Place under a hot grill, skin side down, for 10-12 minutes. Turn over and cook for a further 10 minutes or until the chicken is cooked through and the skin is crisp and golden.
4. Meanwhile, bring the chicken stock to the boil. Add remaining coconut mixture and simmer for 5 minutes. Adjust seasoning.
5. To serve, place a mound of mixed rice in six wide-rimmed soup plates. Add the thickly sliced chicken and ladle over the hot chicken broth. Garnish with red chilli.

57

SPICED CHICKEN WITH CASHEW NUTS

SERVES 8

8 chicken breast fillets, skinned
2.5 cm (1 in) piece of fresh root ginger,
  peeled and roughly chopped
1 × 5 ml tsp coriander seeds
4 cloves
2 × 5 ml tsp black peppercorns
300 ml (10 fl oz) low-fat natural yogurt
1 onion, skinned and roughly chopped
50 g (2 oz) cashew nuts
½ × 5 ml tsp hot chilli powder
2 × 5 ml tsp ground turmeric
40 g (1½ oz) butter
salt
chopped toasted cashew nuts and chopped
  fresh coriander, to garnish

1. Make shallow slashes across each chicken
breast. Put the ginger, coriander seeds, cloves,
peppercorns and yogurt in a blender or food
processor and purée until almost smooth. Pour
the yogurt mixture over the chicken, cover and
leave to marinate in the refrigerator for about
24 hours, turning once.
2. Put the onion, cashew nuts, chilli powder,
turmeric and 150 ml (5 fl oz) water in a blender
or food processor and purée until almost
smooth.
3. Lift the chicken out of the marinade. Melt
the butter in a large frying pan, add the chicken
and fry until browned.
4. Stir the marinade into the frying pan with
the nut mixture and bring slowly to the boil.
Season with salt.
5. Cover the pan and simmer for about
20 minutes, until the chicken is tender, stirring
occasionally. Adjust seasoning. Serve garnished
with cashew nuts and coriander.

COQ AU VIN

SERVES 6-8

1 large chicken, jointed, or 6-8 chicken joints
2 × 15 ml tbs plain flour
salt and pepper
90 g (3½ oz) butter or margarine
115 g (4 oz) lean bacon, diced
1 onion, skinned and quartered
1 carrot, peeled and quartered
4 × 15 ml tbs brandy
600 ml (20 fl oz) red wine
1 garlic clove, skinned and crushed
bouquet garni
1 sugar lump
2 × 15 ml tbs vegetable oil
450 g (1 lb) button onions, skinned
pinch of sugar
1 × 5 ml tsp wine vinegar
225 g (8 oz) button mushrooms, wiped
6 slices of white bread, crusts removed
chopped fresh parsley, to garnish

1. Coat the chicken pieces with half the flour,
liberally seasoned with salt and pepper.
2. Melt 25 g (1 oz) of the butter in a
flameproof casserole, add the chicken pieces
and fry gently until they are golden brown on
all sides. Add the bacon, onion and carrot and
fry until softened.
3. Heat the brandy in a small saucepan, pour
over the chicken and ignite, shaking the pan so
that all the chicken pieces are covered in
flames. Pour on the wine and stir to remove
any sediment from the bottom of the casserole.
Add the garlic, bouquet garni and sugar lump.
Bring to the boil, cover and simmer for 1-1½
hours, until tender.
4. Meanwhile, melt another 25 g (1 oz) of the
butter with 2 × 5 ml tsp of the oil in a frying
pan. Add the button onions and fry until they
begin to brown. Add the sugar and the vinegar,
together with 1 × 15 ml tbs water. Cover and
simmer for 10-15 minutes, until just tender.

5. Melt 25 g (1 oz) of the butter with 2 × 5 ml tsp oil in a pan and add the mushrooms. Cook for a few minutes. Keep warm. Remove chicken from the casserole and place in a serving dish. Surround with the onions and mushrooms. Keep hot.

6. Discard the bouquet garni. Skim the excess fat off the cooking liquid and boil the liquid in the casserole briskly for 3–5 minutes to reduce.

7. Add the remaining oil to the fat in the frying pan and fry the pieces of bread until golden brown on both sides. Cut each slice into triangles or diamonds.

8. Work the remaining flour and butter together to make a beurre manié. Take the casserole off the heat and add the beurre manié in small pieces to the cooking liquid. Stir until smooth, then bring just to the boil. The sauce should now be thick and shiny. Adjust the seasoning and pour over the chicken. Garnish with fried bread and chopped parsley.

VARIATION For Chicken in White Wine, omit the carrot and substitute 300 ml (10 fl oz) chicken stock and 300 ml (10 fl oz) white wine for the red wine.

Coq au Vin

Chicken Kiev

SERVES 4

4 large boneless chicken breasts, skinned
115 g (4 oz) butter, softened
finely grated rind of ½ lemon
1 × 15 ml tbs lemon juice
1 × 15 ml tbs chopped fresh parsley
1 garlic clove, skinned and crushed
salt and pepper
25 g (1 oz) flour
1 × size 3 egg, beaten
115 g (4 oz) fresh white breadcrumbs
vegetable oil for deep frying

1. Place the chicken breasts on a wooden board
and pound them to an even thickness with a
meat mallet or rolling pin.
2. Work the butter with the lemon rind and
juice, the parsley, garlic and salt and pepper to
taste. Place the butter on a sheet of non-stick
or waxed paper and form into a roll.
Refrigerate until the butter is firm.
3. Cut the butter into four pieces and place one
piece on each of the flattened chicken breasts.
Roll up the chicken, folding the ends in to
enclose the butter completely. Secure with
wooden cocktail sticks.
4. Coat the chicken breasts in the seasoned
flour, then in beaten egg and finally in the
breadcrumbs. Pat the crumbs firmly so that the
chicken is well coated. Chill for at least 1 hour
or until required.
5. Heat the oil to 160°C/325°F. Place two
chicken portions in a frying basket and
carefully lower into the oil; deep-fry for about
15 minutes, then drain on absorbent kitchen
paper while frying the rest. Serve immediately.

Roast Chicken in Coconut Sauce

SERVES 4-6

2 × 15 ml tbs oil
1 garlic clove, skinned and crushed
1 × 5 ml tsp each ground coriander, ground
    cumin, ground turmeric, salt, mild chilli powder
1 stalk lemon grass, roughly chopped, or
    grated rind of 1 lemon
225 g (8 oz) onion, skinned and grated
600 ml (20 fl oz) coconut milk
1.4 kg (3 lb) oven-ready chicken
slices of lemon and salad onion, and sprigs of
    coriander, to garnish

1. Mix together the oil, garlic, spices and salt.
Add the lemon grass, onion and a little of the
coconut milk to produce a thick paste.
2. Brush the paste over the chicken inside and
out and place in a roasting tin. Pour over the
remaining coconut milk and place in the oven
at 190°C/375°F/Gas Mark 5 for about 1 hour
20 minutes or until the chicken is golden
brown and tender. To test, pierce the thickest
part of the chicken leg with a skewer. The
juices should be clear, not pink. Baste
occasionally with the coconut milk during
cooking.
3. Remove the chicken. Skim the fat from the
juices in the roasting tin, reheat if necessary and
serve with the chicken. Garnish with slices of
lemon and salad onion and sprigs of coriander.
Accompany with mildly spiced rice.

COOK'S TIP Lemon grass is often used in
Southeast Asian cooking. The bulb may be
sliced or crushed, while the stems may be used
whole, chopped or grated. If you have
difficulty finding lemon grass, fresh lemon may
be used instead.

Roast Chicken in Coconut Sauce

Flaky Duckling Pie

SERVES 6

2 × 15 ml tbs red wine

75 g (3 oz) no-soak pitted prunes,
    roughly chopped

1.8-2 kg (4-4½ lb) oven-ready duckling

salt and pepper

450 g (1 lb) eating apples, peeled, cored,
    quartered and thickly sliced

1 × 15 ml tbs lemon juice

75 g (3 oz) butter, melted

4 sheets filo pastry, 30 × 23 cm (12 × 9 in)
    or 150 g (5 oz) total weight

2 × 15 ml tbs chopped fresh marjoram or
    2 × 5 ml tsp dried

apple slices and fresh coriander, to garnish

1. Spoon the red wine over the prunes, cover
and leave to soak for 2-3 hours.

2. Meanwhile, place the duckling on a rack
over a roasting tin. Prick all over the surface
with a fork and sprinkle lightly with salt. Roast
at 180°C/350°F/Gas Mark for about 1½ hours
or until the duckling is quite tender. Cool,
reserving the fat. Strip the flesh off the
duckling, discarding the skin and the bones and
cut the flesh into bite-size pieces.

3. Heat 3 × 15 ml tbs reserved fat in a sauté
pan. Add the apples and stir-fry for about
5 minutes or until just softening. Take off the
heat, stir in the lemon juice and leave to cool.

4. Brush a 23 cm (9 in) loose-based, fluted flan
tin with butter. Line with one sheet of filo
pastry, allowing the excess pastry to overlap on
one side. Brush butter all over the pastry and
line with two more sheets of filo pastry,
buttering as before. Fill the pie with the pieces
of duckling, prunes, apple slices, marjoram and
seasoning.

5. Fold the pastry over the filling, buttering and
sealing the edges well. Top with the remaining
filo pastry to create a neat top to the pie. Brush
again with melted butter.

6. Stand the tin on a baking tray and bake at
200°C/400°F/Gas Mark 6 for 20-25 minutes
or until crisp and golden. Serve the pie
garnished with apple slices and fresh coriander
leaves.

Norfolk Turkey Breast with Asparagus

SERVES 4

225 g (8 oz) thin asparagus spears

2 turkey breast fillets, each weighing about
    225 g (8 oz), skinned and halved

2 × 15 ml tbs plain flour

salt and pepper

15 g (½ oz) butter

1 × 15 ml tbs vegetable oil

300 ml (10 fl oz) chicken stock

1 × 5 ml tsp chopped fresh sage or
    ½ × 5 ml tsp dried

4 × 15 ml tbs dry white wine

150 ml (5 fl oz) fresh soured cream

1. Cut off the ends of the asparagus if they are
tough and woody. Trim them all to the same
length, cut off the tips and cut the stalks into
three pieces.

2. Pound each turkey breast lightly with a
rolling pin or meat mallet. Coat in the flour
seasoned with salt and pepper, shaking off any
excess. Heat the butter and oil in a large frying
pan and fry the turkey until lightly browned on
both sides. Add the chicken stock, asparagus
stalks, reserving the tips, the sage and wine,
cover and cook gently for 15-20 minutes, until
tender.

3. Five minutes before the end of the cooking
time, add the reserved asparagus tips and the
cream. Season to taste. Serve with new
potatoes.

Norfolk Turkey Breast with Asparagus

BALLONTINE OF TURKEY

SERVES ABOUT 20

butter or margarine
225 g (8 oz) onion, skinned and roughly chopped
225 g (8 oz) button mushrooms, chopped
2 large garlic cloves, skinned and crushed
675 g (1½ lb) pork sausagemeat
115 g (4 oz) fresh breadcrumbs
6 × 15 ml tbs chopped fresh parsley
4 × 15 ml tbs Dijon mustard
grated rind and juice of 1 lemon
1 × size 3 egg, beaten
salt and pepper
5.5 kg (12 lb) turkey, boned (see page 67)
450 g (1 lb) smoked loin of pork

1. Heat 50 g (2 oz) butter in a sauté pan and fry the onion until light brown. Increase the heat, mix in the mushrooms and garlic and fry until all excess liquid has evaporated. Place in a large bowl and cool.
2. Stir the sausagemeat, breadcrumbs, parsley, mustard, lemon rind and lemon juice, the egg and plenty of seasoning into the mushroom mixture. Beat thoroughly.
3. Lay the boned turkey flat on a board, flesh side up, and spread this stuffing mixture over the flesh. Place the smoked loin (cut in half lengthways if necessary) on top and then fold the turkey skin around to enclose the stuffing completely. Secure with fine skewers.
4. Spread the turkey with butter and season. Wrap in foil and place in a roasting tin.
5. Bake at 180°C/350°F/Gas Mark 4 for 2½ hours. Fold back the foil and return to the oven for about 1 hour or until well browned. Test with a fine skewer; if it is cooked, the juices should run clear.
6. Lift onto a serving plate and cool for about 20 minutes before slicing thickly to serve, or cool completely, cover and chill before slicing.

Ballontine of Turkey

GLAZED STUFFED TURKEY WITH FORCEMEAT BALLS

SERVES ABOUT 10-12

3 × 15 ml tbs oil

butter or margarine

335 g (12 oz) onion, skinned and roughly chopped

6 celery sticks, roughly chopped

2 eating apples, quartered, cored and roughly chopped

175 g (6 oz) fresh breadcrumbs

115 g (4 oz) coarse oatmeal

50 g (2 oz) suet

3 × 15 ml tbs fresh chopped sage or
   1 × 5 ml tsp dried, rubbed sage

finely grated rind and juice of 2 oranges

salt and pepper

1 × size 3 egg, beaten

about 5 kg (11 lb) oven-ready turkey

3 × 15 ml tbs thick honey

3 × 15 ml tbs dry sherry

about 450 ml (16 fl oz) turkey or chicken stock

4 × 15 ml tbs cornflour

fresh herbs or watercress, to garnish

FORCEMEAT BALLS:

50 g (2 oz) butter or margarine

175 g (6 oz) onion, skinned and roughly chopped

50 g (2 oz) walnut pieces, chopped

½ × 5 ml tsp chilli powder

900 g (2 lb) pork sausages or sausagemeat

8 × 15 ml tbs chopped fresh parsley

salt and pepper

flour

oil

Glazed Stuffed Turkey with Forcemeat Balls

1. Heat the oil in a frying pan. Add 50 g (2 oz) butter and fry the onion and celery until beginning to brown. Stir the apples into the pan and fry for a minute or two. Turn out into a large bowl to cool.

2. Stir in the breadcrumbs, oatmeal, suet and sage. Add the orange rind with half the juice. Season well, add the egg and mix thoroughly.

3. Spoon the stuffing into the neck end of the turkey only. Secure the flap of skin with a fine skewer. Place remaining stuffing in a greased ovenproof dish to bake later.

4. Place the turkey on a strong sheet of foil, then lift into a large roasting tin. Spread the breast and legs thinly with the honey. Dot generously with butter and grind over some black pepper. Carefully spoon over the sherry and fold the foil loosely around the turkey to enclose completely.

5. Bake at 180°C/350°F/Gas Mark 4 for about 4 hours. Fold the foil back, baste well and return to the oven for about a further 1 hour. (Put the dish of stuffing in the oven to bake for the final hour.) The turkey should be a rich dark brown. Test the thickest part of the leg with a fine skewer; the juices should run clear when the bird is cooked. Return to the oven for a little longer, if necessary, laying a sheet of foil over the bird, once it is well browned.

6. Meanwhile, make the forcemeat balls. Heat the butter in a frying pan. Add the onion and fry until beginning to brown. Mix in the nuts and chilli powder and stir-fry for 1 minute. Turn out onto a plate. Allow to cool.

7. If necessary, split open the sausages, then place all the sausagemeat in a bowl. Stir in the cold onions with half the parsley. Season well. With floured hands shape the sausagemeat into about 32 balls. Place on a flat baking sheet, cover and chill.

8. About 30 minutes before the turkey comes out of the oven, heat a thin film of oil in a large roasting tin. Add the sausagemeat balls. Bake at 180°C/350°F/Gas Mark 4 for about 45 minutes, turning occasionally. Drain on kitchen paper before tossing quickly in remaining parsley.

9. Lift the turkey onto a serving dish, when it is cooked, cover and keep warm for 20-30 minutes. Pour the cooking liquor into a saucepan and skim well. Add the stock with the remaining orange juice and bubble for 4-5 minutes to reduce slightly and strengthen the flavour.

10. Mix the cornflour to a smooth paste with a little water. Stir into the pan juices and bring to the boil. Cook for a minute or two. If necessary, thicken further before adjusting seasoning. Garnish the turkey with fresh herbs or watercress and serve with forcemeat balls.

BONING A BIRD

1. Place the bird breast-side down on a large chopping board. Using a small sharp knife, cut straight along the backbone. Gradually fillet the flesh away from the carcass, keeping the knife as close to the bones as possible. Take great care not to puncture the skin during filleting as it has to act as a 'case' for the roast bird – if the skin is split, the stuffing will burst out as the joint roasts.

2. Loosen the leg and wing ball-and-socket joints with the point of the knife. Push these joints away from the carcass until they loosen and partially come away. Carefully split the leg flesh and ease out the bones and sinews. Ease out the large wing joint, reserving the small wing tips for the stock pot. Run your fingers all over the flesh to ensure there are no bones or sinews remaining.

3. If you are boning a turkey for a ballontine, fillet most of the leg and thigh meat from one side of the bird and trim any excessively fat portions of breast flesh – you should have about 900 g (2 lb) trimmed meat to use in casseroles.

BONED TURKEY WITH CRANBERRY STUFFING

SERVES 10-12

2 × 170 g packets stuffing mix,
   preferably chestnut
175 g (6 oz) fresh or frozen cranberries
175 g (6 oz) walnut pieces or pecan nuts
2 lemons
8 × 15 ml tbs chopped fresh parsley
salt and pepper
4.5 kg (10 lb) oven-ready turkey, boned
   (see page 67)
225 g (8 oz) rindless smoked back bacon
50 g (2 oz) butter, softened

1. Prepare the stuffing mix as instructed, but
use only about three–quarters of the quantity of
water; cool. Stir in cranberries, walnuts, grated
lemon rind and parsley. Season well.
2. Place turkey skin-side down and lay the
bacon across the flesh; pile the stuffing in the
centre.
3. Tuck the neck end over the filling, draw the
long sides of the bird over the stuffing and sew
up with fine string to encase completely.
Skewer into a neater shape if wished. (Don't
roll up too tightly or you'll find that the bird
will burst during cooking.) Weigh the bird.
4. Place turkey breast-side up on foil in a
roasting tin. Spread with butter; season. Pour
over the juice of one lemon. Wrap over foil to
make a parcel.
5. Roast at 180°C/350°F/Gas Mark 4 for
15 minutes per 450 g (1 lb), then remove from
oven. Raise the oven temperature to
200°C/400°F/Gas Mark 6. Unwrap the turkey
and return to the oven for a further 30 minutes
to brown, basting occasionally. Test with a fine
skewer. If the juices run clear the bird is
cooked; if not, return to oven for a little longer.
6. Leave to rest for at least 15 minutes before
carving. Serve hot or cold.

BONED TURKEY WITH CHICKEN LIVER MOUSSE

SERVES 8

115 g (4 oz) unsalted butter
450 g (1 lb) chicken livers, trimmed
1 eating apple, peeled, cored and roughly chopped
75 g (3 oz) rindless streaky bacon,
   roughly chopped
1 small onion, skinned and roughly chopped
3 × 15 ml tbs chopped fresh tarragon or
   ½ × 5 ml tsp dried
4 × 15 ml tbs dry sherry
salt and pepper
two boneless turkey breasts, each weighing
   675 g (1½ lb)
3 × 15 ml tbs chopped fresh parsley
24 pistachio nuts, shelled and skinned
mixed salad leaves (radicchio lettuce, lamb's
   lettuce, frisée, endive, etc) and fresh poached
   and cooked cranberries, to serve

1. Melt half the butter in a large sauté pan and
brown the chicken livers well on all sides.
2. Return the livers to the pan with the apple,
bacon, onion and tarragon. Stir together over a
high heat for about 5 minutes. Remove from
the heat and stir in the sherry, then leave to
cool.
3. Blend the mixture in a blender or food
processor with the remaining butter. Press it all
through a fine sieve into a bowl and season to
taste. Cover the dish with cling film and chill
well for 30 minutes.
4. Skin the turkey breasts and remove the false
fillets (the loose piece of flesh underneath) from
each one. Place all the turkey pieces between
two sheets of damp greaseproof paper and bat
out the flesh with a rolling pin to make
thinner, flatter pieces.
5. Place one of the larger turkey pieces on a
sheet of buttered foil. Sprinkle with 1 × 15 ml
tbs chopped fresh parsley. Spread one-third of

the chicken liver mousse over the parsley and dot over the top with one-third of the nuts.

6. Place one of the false fillets on top and repeat the parsley, mousse and pistachio layers. Add the remaining false fillet and repeat the layers as before. Finish with the remaining large piece of turkey. Tie the whole turkey together securely at 2.5 cm (1 in) intervals with fine string. Wrap tightly in a double layer of foil and place in a baking tin.

7. Cook at 190°C/375°F/Gas Mark 5 for about 1½ hours or until the juices run clear. Carefully pour off any excess fat. Place the wrapped turkey joint in a 900 g (2 lb) loaf tin. Cover with foil and weight down. When cool enough, place in the refrigerator and leave overnight.

8. To serve, turn out of the tin, unwrap, slice thickly and serve with mixed salad leaves and fresh poached and cooled cranberries.

Boned Turkey with Cranberry Stuffing

CARAMELISED DUCKLING

SERVES 10

8–10 x 15 ml tbs olive oil
1.4 kg (3 lb) onions, skinned, halved and sliced
75 g (3 oz) soft light brown sugar
6 × 15 ml tbs sherry vinegar
12 whole allspice berries
10 duckling breasts, about 1.8 kg (4 lb)
    total weight
50 g (2 oz) white plain flour
2 × 5 ml tsp paprika
salt and pepper
900 ml (1½ pt) chicken stock
4 × 5 ml tsp dry sherry
grated rind and juice of 1 lemon
2 × 5 ml tsp chopped fresh marjoram or
    1 × 5 ml tsp dried
175 g (6 oz) Parma ham, chopped
flat-leaf parsley, to garnish

1. Heat 2 × 15 ml tbs oil in a large flameproof casserole. Add the onions and sauté, uncovered, for 20 minutes. Stir in the next three ingredients. Cook for about 5 minutes, until caramelised and a rich brown.
2. Meanwhile, skin the duckling and cut into bite-size pieces. Mix the flour and paprika; season. Coat the duckling in the flour.
3. Remove the onions and juices, rinse the pan and add 5 × 15 ml tbs oil. Heat, then brown the duckling in batches, adding a little more oil if necessary. Drain on absorbent kitchen paper. Place all the duckling pieces back in the casserole with any remaining flour. Off the heat, stir in the stock with the onions, sherry, lemon rind and juice, and marjoram. Bring to the boil, cover and cook at 150°C/300°F/Gas Mark 2 for 50 minutes or until almost tender.
4. Lightly sauté the Parma ham in 1 × 15 ml tbs oil for 3-4 minutes. Stir into the duckling. Cover and cook for a further 10 minutes or until the duckling is tender. Season and garnish with flat-leaf parsley.

BONED DUCKLING WITH LEMON MUSHROOM STUFFING

SERVES 6-8

40 g (1½ oz) butter or margarine
115 g (4 oz) onion, skinned and finely chopped
1 garlic clove, skinned and crushed
75 g (3 oz) button mushrooms, trimmed and
    finely chopped
115 g (4 oz) ham, in one piece, diced
1 bunch of watercress, finely chopped
175 g (6oz) minced pork
75 g (3 oz) fresh white breadcrumbs
2 lemons
1 egg and 1 egg yolk
salt and pepper
2 kg (4½ lb) oven-ready duckling, boned
    (see page 67)
watercress, celery tops and orange or lemon rind
    strips, to garnish

1. Melt butter in a medium pan and sauté the onion, garlic and mushrooms for 4-5 minutes until most of the liquid has evaporated. Cool.
2. In a medium bowl, mix together the ham, watercress, pork, breadcrumbs, grated lemon rind and 2 × 15 ml tbs strained lemon juice. Stir in the onion and mushroom mixture, then beat in the egg, egg yolk and seasoning.
3. Pile the stuffing down the centre of the duckling and pat into a sausage shape. Fold the flesh over the stuffing to enclose completely and sew up neatly with needle and cotton.
4. Put the duckling on a wire rack over a roasting tin. Prick lightly with a skewer and sprinkle with a little salt. Cook at 200°C/400°F/ Gas Mark 6 for about 1½ hours or until the juices run clear. Garnish and serve.

Boned Duckling with Lemon Mushroom Stuffing

CIRCASSIAN CHICKEN DRUMSTICKS

MAKES 16

16 chicken drumsticks
115 g (4 oz) shelled walnuts, roughly chopped
150 ml (5 fl oz) tomato ketchup
4 × 15 ml tbs soft brown sugar
5 × 15 ml tbs wine vinegar
2 × 5 ml tsp chilli powder
2 × 5 ml tsp celery salt
black pepper
300 ml (10 fl oz) chicken stock

1. With a sharp knife, score the skin of the drumsticks right through to the flesh. Place in a single layer in a shallow dish.
2. Mix together all the remaining ingredients, except the stock. Pour over the drumsticks, cover and leave to marinate in the refrigerator for 24 hours, turning the drumsticks over and coating with the marinade occasionally.
3. Place the drumsticks on the grid of a preheated barbecue and cook for 15-20 minutes, turning from time to time.
4. Meanwhile, transfer the marinade to a heavy saucepan, pour in the stock and bring to the boil, stirring. Lower the heat and simmer until reduced slightly, stirring occasionally. Serve the drumsticks warm, with the marinade handed separately in a jug.

VARIATION Circassian dishes invariably have nuts in their ingredients. Walnuts are given here, but you could use almonds or hazelnuts, or a mixture of two or three different nuts.

Circassian Chicken Drumsticks

LIME PEPPERED CHICKEN

SERVES 8

6 skinless chicken breast fillets, cut into
    bite-size pieces
2 small yellow or red chillies, thinly sliced
2 × 5 ml tsp coarse-ground black peppercorns
grated or shredded rind and juice of 3 limes
1 garlic clove, skinned and crushed
2 × 15 ml tbs clear honey
small aubergines or slices of courgette or
    onion, to finish

1. Toss together the chicken, chillies and the
next four ingredients. Cover and marinate in
the refrigerator for at least 10 minutes.
2. Thread the chicken onto metal or wooden
skewers. Thread an aubergine half, a slice of
courgette or a wedge of onion onto the
skewers to finish. Cook on the barbecue or
under a hot grill for 10–12 minutes; turn
frequently, basting with marinade. Serve with
Spicy Dipping Sauce (see right).

COOK'S TIP When preparing chillies, it's a
good idea to wear rubber gloves as the chillies
can irritate the skin.

SPICY DIPPING SAUCE

4 × 15 ml tbs mango chutney
1 garlic clove, skinned and crushed
2.5 cm (1 in) piece of fresh root ginger, peeled
    and grated
2 × 5 ml tsp light, soft brown sugar
2 × 5 ml tsp white wine vinegar
3 × 15 ml tbs soy sauce
few drops of Tabasco sauce
6 × 15 ml tbs oil
small, mixed chillies, to garnish

1. Place all the ingredients in a food processor
and blend for about 15 seconds or until well
combined. Serve garnished with a few chillies.

Lime Peppered Chicken

BARBECUED CHICKEN

SERVES 4

1.4 kg (3 lb) chicken, quartered or jointed
1 quantity marinade of your choice (see below)
melted butter

1. Put the chicken pieces in a dish and pour the marinade over them. Leave for 2 hours.
2. Pour a little melted butter on each chicken joint and place on the barbecue grid over very hot coals. Brown quickly on all sides then remove from the grid and place each joint on a 38 cm (15 in) square piece of foil. Wrap round the chicken and seal the edges securely. Place each packet on the grid and cook for a further 20 minutes, turning once.
3. Heat the marinade and serve separately as a sauce. Serve the chicken in the foil packets so that none of the buttery juices are lost.

MARINADES

BASIC MARINADE
grated rind and juice of 1 lemon
2 garlic cloves, skinned and crushed
115 g (4 oz) onion, skinned and grated
1 × 5 ml tsp chopped fresh basil or thyme
4 × 15 ml tbs olive oil
salt and pepper

Whisk together all the ingredients. Pour over meat, ensuring all pieces are coated. Cover and marinate for as long as possible. Use remaining marinade as a baste for cooking.

CHILLI MARINADE
330 g bottle mild chilli relish
1 × 5 ml tsp salt
2 × 5 ml tsp dried horseradish
1 garlic clove, skinned and quartered
115 ml (4 fl oz) wine vinegar

Mix all the marinade ingredients in a large dish. Add the chicken pieces and coat well. Cover and refrigerate for at least 2 hours, turning from time to time.

ORANGE HERB MARINADE
150 ml (5 fl oz) white wine or dry vermouth
3 × 15 ml tbs olive oil
juice of 2 oranges
1 × 5 ml tsp each chopped fresh rosemary,
    thyme and marjoram
1 garlic clove, skinned and crushed

Mix the ingredients in a shallow dish and stir until well blended. Spoon over the chicken and marinate for at least 2 hours.

LIME MARINADE
115 ml (4 fl oz) lime juice
3 × 15 ml tbs vegetable oil
1 × 15 ml tbs grated lime rind
4 × 5 ml tsp salt
¼ × 5 ml tsp crushed peppercorns

Mix the ingredients in a shallow dish and stir until well blended. Spoon over the chicken and marinate for at least 2 hours.

SALAD ONION AND SOY MARINADE
115 g (4 fl oz) soy sauce
2 × 15 ml tbs dry sherry
50 g (2 oz) salad onions, trimmed and
    thinly sliced
2 × 15 ml tbs soft light brown sugar
½ × 5 ml tsp salt
½ × 5 ml tsp ground ginger

Mix the ingredients in a shallow dish and blend well. Spoon over the chicken and marinate for at least 2 hours.

CHICKEN NIBBLES

SERVES 6

335 g (12 oz) boneless chicken fillet or thighs,
   cut into thin strips
1 × size 3 egg, lightly beaten
5 × 15 ml tbs sage and onion stuffing mix
oil

1. Dip the chicken strips in the beaten egg,
then coat thoroughly with the stuffing mix.
Cover and refrigerate for about 15 minutes.
2. Brush the chicken pieces with oil and cook
on the barbecue grid for about 8 minutes,
turning frequently. Brush with a little more oil
during the cooking if needed.

CHICKEN WITH BASIL SAUCE

SERVES 4

bunch of basil, about 50 g (2 oz)
4 chicken breasts with skin, about
   175 g (6 oz) each
6 anchovy fillets
4 × 15 ml tbs red wine vinegar
4 × 5 ml tsp Dijon mustard
175 ml (6 fl oz) olive oil

1. Carefully push 2–3 basil leaves under the
skin of each chicken breast.
2. Place the remaining basil leaves, anchovy
fillets, vinegar and mustard in a food processor
and blend until the mixture becomes quite

Chicken with Basil Sauce

smooth. With the motor still running, slowly pour in the olive oil. Transfer the mixture to a small bowl.

3. Cook the chicken breasts on the barbecue for about 6-8 minutes each side, or until they are cooked through. (If you are using boneless chicken, it will not take quite so long to cook.) Serve with a few spoonfuls of the basil sauce and accompanied by pasta.

CHICKEN AND BACON KEBABS

SERVES 4

8 thin rashers streaky bacon, rinded
about 335 g (12 oz) chicken breast fillets, skinned and cut into bite-size pieces
1 small pineapple, peeled, cored and roughly chopped into bite-size pieces
1 quantity Basic Marinade (see page 75)
Instant Barbecue Sauce (see right), to serve

1. Stretch the bacon rashers with the back of a round-bladed knife and cut in half. Wrap each chicken piece in bacon.
2. Thread the chicken and bacon rolls onto long metal skewers together with the pineapple pieces.
3. Place the skewers in a shallow, non-metallic dish and pour the marinade over them. Cover and leave to marinate for as long as possible.
4. Cook the kebabs on the barbecue for about 8-10 minutes, turning regularly and basting occasionally with the marinade. Serve with Instant Barbecue Sauce.

VARIATION Use liver instead of chicken, and sliced onions instead of pineapple pieces. This is an unusual and delicious way of serving the traditional combination of liver and bacon.

INSTANT BARBECUE SAUCE

1 garlic clove, skinned and roughly chopped
salt and pepper
½ × 5 ml tsp paprika
pinch of chilli powder
4 × 15 ml tbs each clear honey, tomato ketchup, orange juice, red wine vinegar and soy sauce

Place all the ingredients in a blender or food processor and blend. Serve cold or simmer for 5 minutes to serve hot.

CHICKEN AND GRAPE WHOLEMEAL PITTAS

MAKES 8

5 × 15 ml tbs low-fat mayonnaise
5 × 15 ml tbs low-fat natural yogurt
50 g (2 oz) celery, thinly sliced
50 g (2 oz) cashew nuts, toasted
225 g (8 oz) cooked chicken or turkey, cut into bite-size pieces
115 g (4 oz) small seedless green grapes, halved if wished
salt and pepper
8 small wholemeal pitta breads
4 iceberg lettuce leaves, shredded

1. Mix the mayonnaise with the yogurt and stir in the celery, nuts, chicken and grapes. Season to taste.
2. Split each pitta along one side, spoon in some shredded lettuce and fill with the chicken and grape mixture. Wrap each parcel in clingfilm or foil.

CHICKEN PARCELS

SERVES 4

15 g (½ oz) butter
I small onion, skinned and chopped
2 carrots, peeled and diced
I × 15 ml tbs plain wholemeal flour
I × 5 ml tsp mild curry powder
300 ml (10 fl oz) chicken stock
I × 5 ml tsp lemon juice
225 g (8 oz) boneless cooked chicken, chopped
salt and pepper
340 g chilled puff pastry,
beaten egg, to glaze

1. Melt the butter in a large saucepan, add the onion and carrots, then cover and cook for 4–5 minutes, until the onion is transparent. Stir in the flour and curry powder and cook, stirring, for 1 minute. Remove from the heat and gradually add the stock. Bring to the boil, stirring continuously, then simmer for 2–3 minutes, until thickened.
2. Reduce the heat, add the lemon juice and chicken and season to taste. Leave to cool.
3. When the chicken mixture is cool, roll out the pastry on a lightly floured surface to a 35 cm (14 in) square. Using a sharp knife, cut into 4 squares.
4. Place the pastry on dampened baking trays, then spoon the chicken mixture on to one half of the pastry, leaving a border round the edges. Brush the edges of each square lightly with water. Fold each square in half and seal and crimp the edges to make a parcel.
5. Make 2 small slashes on the top of each parcel. Brush with beaten egg to glaze.
6. Bake at 220°C/425°F/Gas Mark 7 for 15–20 minutes or until the pastry is golden brown. Allow to cool before packing in a rigid container.

VARIATION These parcels can also be served hot, with a salad or Brussels sprouts.

DEVILLED CHICKEN DRUMSTICKS

MAKES 6

150 ml (5 fl oz) vegetable oil
I × 5 ml tsp mild curry powder
I × 5 ml tsp paprika
½ × 5 ml tsp ground allspice
½ × 5 ml tsp ground ginger
6 chicken drumsticks

1. Whisk together the oil and spices to make the marinade.
2. Skin the chicken drumsticks then, using a sharp knife, make 3 shallow slashes in the flesh of each one. Spoon the marinade over the chicken, cover and chill in the refrigerator for 4–5 hours, turning occasionally.
3. Place the chicken drumsticks in a roasting tin just large enough to hold them in a single layer. Pour over the marinade. Bake in the oven at 200°C/400°F/Gas Mark 6 for 40–45 minutes, basting frequently and turning once. Cool on a wire rack.
4. When completely cool, wrap a little foil over the end of each drumstick, or top with a cutlet frill. Pack together in a rigid container for transporting.

COOK'S TIP Marinating is an easy and convenient way of flavouring and tenderising chicken. Frozen chicken must be completely thawed before placing it in the marinade so that it can absorb the flavours. Making slash marks in it helps improve the absorption process. Remember, chicken should be kept in the marinade for at least 4 hours; the longer it soaks, the better.

Chicken Parcels